M000317156

JC QUINTANA

Serious Relationships

THE

7

ELEMENTS

OF

SUCCESSFUL

BUSINESS

RELATIONSHIPS

Printed in the United States of America.

Serious Relationhips: The Seven Elements of Successful Business
Relationships

CRG PRESS'

Kennesaw, Georgia. United States

ISBN 978-0-9889145-5-1 (pbk.)

ISBN 978-0-9889145-4-4 (hc.)

1st Edition June 2017

To all my

Serious Relationship

at home,

at work,

and in life...

CONTENT

"Give me more than a reason to do business with you... give me a reason to care... "

Are you in a serious relationship?

Andy loves people. I mean, REALLY cares about people. He may be, by far, the most genuine person I have ever met. Andrew and I worked together, supporting the channel alliance and partner programs of a technology company in Phoenix, Arizona many years ago. The company, a fast-growing startup founded by customer industry pioneer Pat Sullivan, was enjoying some very steady growth, and many independent technology implementers had joined as resellers.

In total, Andy and I supported over four hundred independent partner companies across the world. I cannot prove this, but I am convinced that Andy knew every person, at every one of those companies by first and last name. That is what I respect most about him. Despite geography or language (and Andy speaks at least five fluently) he always took the time to know people's interests and needs personally. His multilingual skills allowed him to jump in and out of conversations with international partners, listening intently to their problems, stopping along the way to ask about their business and family. When English was not personal enough, he would speak to them in theirs. I do not mean only in "their language" (as in idiom), I mean in THEIR language; the way they needed to be heard and with the words that meant something to them. What I found interesting about Andy, is that his attitude and personal devotion to serving others extended to customers and employees. Not just the partners he supported. To Andy, these were not "business" relationships; they were "serious" relationships. They were equally worthy of his time and focus because to him they represented a connection as serious and important as those in his personal life. Even more memorable is that Andy treated customers and team members within the company with the same level of value, engagement, and empathy. I have not worked with Andy for many years. We do not even live in the same continent anymore. Yet, every Christmas I get a greeting card with a special message from him.

The world has changed a lot since I last saw Andy. Looking back after all these years of evolution in customer technology implementation and practice, it is ironic to see so much of it disconnected from its original purpose. Andy and I helped build some of the first-generation customer relationship management applications that gave way to today's modern customer technology. Frankly, I did not expect the technology that helps automate our interactions with people to astonish me in their elegance and high functionality. However, I could never have predicted that in the process of building tools to facilitate a more human connection with people, that we would have lost the skills to do so. It feels like the investment in automation has made us lazy in the areas that matter.

We can automate almost every aspect of recruiting, hiring, onboarding, and managing employees. Most companies can automate most of the processes required to onboard a new customer or employee. Most every aspect of customer service is digital across social, mobility, analytics, and cloud technology. Digital transformation is the emerging strategy for many companies. Most customers can use automation to learn, buy, or get service from your company. Yet, it seems like the tools we created to move relationship impediments out of the way have become impediments themselves.

We have become servants to the tools of service intended to give us more time to build genuine relationships with real people (tools that were supposed to make more time for us to have quality human interactions). While becoming more technologically proficient, and transitioning human tasks to technology, we lost the skills needed to win and keep relationships; the very foundation of business. We use words like relationship, engagement, loyalty, and service to describe goals and practices that are human, but that represent transactions that never lead to anything close to what we call them. The digital tools intended to facilitate a more human business environment have replaced our heart with a digital heart; one that beats mechanically within our companies.

Are you in a serious relationship? A strange question to ask at the very beginning of a business book, I know. Nonetheless, I ask you to consider the first thing that came to mind when I asked you that question.

Are you in a serious relationship? Have you ever been? Are you now or hope to be in a serious relationship?

Of the hundreds of people to whom I have asked this question, only a handful have connected the question to a business, versus personal, situation. Almost all respondents have referenced a spouse or girlfriend or personal love interest. Most referred to a significant other with whom they have a formal or legal agreement they see as a "commitment." The question is usually met with surprise even if I ask it in a social setting, but even more so when I ask that question at a business event.

When I get people to engage in the "serious relationship" conversation (usually prompted by curiosity) I ask the question again in a slightly different way. I ask, "Are you in a serious relationship with your customers?" "How about your employees?" "How about your business partners (such as your value-added resellers and distributors)?" Asking questions like these results in a lot of puzzled expressions and very lively conversations for sure.

Why is it so easy to connect the words "serious" and "relationship" in your personal life, but so difficult to attach the sentiment to your business life. After all, we spend most of our day at work in situations that mirror the emotional intensity and emotional bond of our personal relationships. People work at the same office and with the same people for years. You maintain the same long-term relationships with customers and business partners regardless of where your career takes you.

So why does it feel different? Why does it have to BE different? I have been asking myself these questions for a while. Why do people have such difficulty with this association? I mean, I get it. You do not use the word "serious relationship" at work as a standard. It is more something you say when your best friend tells you that, after seeing this person for a few months, they are going on a cruise together. Or you hear them talking about a future together. "Wow," you say, "that relationship is getting SERIOUS."

However, the word serious is not exclusive to personal relationships. Neither is the word relationship, for that matter. So why don't we inject this idea into our business vernacular? Customer relationships (for example) go from "casual" or "distant" and "interested" to "serious" in their progression from prospect to customer. This, by the way, is why when a salesperson tells me that they are going to visit a prospective client I ask, "Is it serious?" It makes the point. After all, serious relationships suggest commitment and longevity and that is what we all want from customers. We also want our employees to love where they work and stay with our company. We want business partners and stakeholders who support and distribute our products and services to be as exclusive as possible too.

I do not dispute that the ideas of loyalty and formality have changed over time and that not every interaction with people leads to a serious business relationship. Being with a company for a couple of years is not an automatic indicator that the employee plans to stay or the employer plans to keep them. The field of organizational psychology is heavily vested in the study of psychological contracts companies break with people all the time and I know it is a subject that deserves mindful attention. Companies also switch vendors all the time based on economic factors that have nothing to do with the length or strength of the relationship. Nevertheless, the question remains about the way we view relationships with people outside our immediate and intimate personal relationships.

I will ask you again... are you in a serious relationship with your customers, employees, and partners? I hope the question motivates you to evaluate your perception of your business relationships and the level of genuine attention and investment you demonstrate towards them. I hope it persuades you to ask, right from the beginning of this book, if your business relationships rank as "serious" in your mindset, behavior, and focus.

Not all your business relationships are going to end up as serious relationships any more than you call every interaction with people a serious relationship. You will learn early in this book that one of the reasons we do not care properly for the relationships that matter is that we are too busy with the relationships we should have never been a part of. As a result, the relationships we should make serious do not get the attention they deserve as frequently and consistently as they should. Business relationships suffer from neglect too, just as personal relationships do. They suffer from a kind of neglectful segregation that delegates its definition and maintenance to different people and organizations throughout the company. Some people care for the definition of the relationship, others with how to communicate, and yet others with how to keep that relationship mutually beneficial.

The people who manage customer relationships do all these separate from those who manage employee or partner relationships. Each relationship "type" represents a bucket of effort and investment we manage in isolation. You manage each relationship type differently. You rank its importance based on how critical it is to generate revenue. At times, you even struggle to choose which one deserves the most immediate attention while trying to qualify your investment (of money, time, and effort) by always connecting it back to how it will help you generate money from customers. This is where all the dialog about ranking the customer first or the employee first comes from.

Under this model, the people, infrastructure, and resources that build strategies and implement technologies to win and support each of these business relationships do so (for the most part) in silos. The people who manage your customer relationships use words like customer experience, customer engagement, and customer service, to describe the way they win and keep customers. Within the same company, the people responsible for employee recruitment and retention talk about employee retention, development, and reducing churn. Elsewhere, yet another group of people measure trust and transparency in their interactions with external channels. They care about the companies that sell and distribute your products and services to customer and employees on your behalf.

The people who care about customers, employees, and partners are all important. They build the relationships that build your business. Most of them do so in seclusion. All of them compete for attention and budget to make it all work. If these were the relationship dynamics of a family, trying to work together to influence separate aspects of a child's life, it would be a very dysfunctional family indeed. Each member of the family would have different norms and even approaches for providing what the child needs, make it easy for them to get what they need, and care for their emotional health.

In the process, our practices and even our perception of what it takes to manage a business relationship become less interrelated. We begin to think that the methods are different for managing serious customer relationships from the serious employee and partner relationships. Yes, it is true that customer organizations have a different mandate and operate differently from employee and HR or channel alliances programs. In that sense, we must remain aware of our operational differences. Nevertheless, why have we developed completely different programs and methodologies for caring about the basic needs of people simply because they are a customer, or a partner, or an employee? Are the needs of your business relationships not alike at the core? Can leveraging what you understand about successful relationships improve how you build the relationships that build your business, collectively? Can managing expectations, building engagement and participation, making people feel special, keeping your promises, showing empathy, trust, and giving people what they need, all apply to the customer, employee, or partner relationships alike? The answer is a resounding YES!

This book is about concepts we have abandoned or disconnected from in response to the daily pressures that entangle us in both business and personal life. Like with interpersonal relationships, business relationships take skill and investment and collaboration to make them successful. My hope is that you come back to this book for guidance often and that you will use it frequently to remind yourself of the methods that increase connection across all your business relationships.

This book represents a maturity model developed to assess the health of your business relationships. It provides seven relationship elements, which all your business relationships need to subsist. We call them elements of the "serious relationship" because they are found together in relationships that stay committed through difficulty, work together to improve the relationship; and prevent deterioration. The seven elements are not a taxonomy or hierarchy, although I talk at length about building on "definition" and measuring "experience" as a foundation for the other elements. The seven elements of serious relationships are:

Definition: People want to understand the value, risks, and rewards involved in a business relationship. They want to comprehend the rules, boundaries, and expectations of the relationship in a clearly defined way before making contented commitments.

Engagement: People need to communicate through the channels most important to them, and that communication must have a positive climate and level of participation. They want to understand value creation and their role in that process before they will collaborate in the value creation process.

Centricity: People need you to make them feel like they are the center of your decisions. The engagement I just told you about must be personalized to their needs. They must feel relevant and preferential in your decision-making before they make concessions.

Responsibility: All your business relationships need you to keep your promises proactively. They need to know you have the knowledge and ability to fulfill your role AND that you are reliable and credible to do so.

Accountability: People also need to know that in those times when you are not obligated to do something, that you will still be responsive to their individual needs. Even more than empathy, people want you to be responsive to what matters to them.

Transparency: People need accessibility and visibility into your decisions, thinking, and actions. Transparency allows them to see the level of consistency that leads to trust. Trust leads to the level of interdependence and self-disclosure that keep relationships together. However, transparency allows people to trust you in specific areas, even if they do not trust you in all areas.

Staging: Experiences (individual and collective) require intentional guidance and environmental preparation. People frame the value they are getting from a relationship against the landscape of their experiences. They recollect a single interaction or history of interactions with you and ask, "did I get what I needed?" "did you make it easy for me to get what I needed?" and "did I connect emotionally?" Therefore, relationships require that you are strategic in the staging of those experiences based on the type of relationship you are trying to develop.

The great news about these seven elements is that you are already acquainted with them. You already define the norms of your relationships with significant others to ensure the relationship is fair and equitable. You communicate with the special people in your life through the channels that align with your lifestyle, geography, and even technology preference (some of us like to speak in person while others text). Your values and culture are already at the center of your successful relationships. You learn the skills required to be more responsible to your children and loved ones. You seek and demonstrate empathy to others. You know that transparency leads to trust. And you know that setting the perfect table at Thanksgiving isn't about the turkey, but about the memories it creates (and OK, maybe a little bit about the turkey). This book helps you bring these concepts into your professional business life, and apply them to your relationships with all business stakeholders.

I urge you to give the ideas of this book a chance. Think about the importance of the relationships that keep your business healthy. Not only your customer relationships, but the other relationships that allow you to deliver your value proposition to the right customer segments, through the right channels, resources, and activities. Think about the indisputable interdependence that connects your customer, employee and partner relationships with equal and mutual benefit. Think about opportunities to collaborate and turn silos into highly functional organizations that support a common vision of building business relationships through common methods. Think about the role of technology to support that vision, and where critical decision-making needs to correct and support the use of technology tools. Think about the value of measuring all your business relationships (not just customer relationships) based on functionality, accessibility, and emotion.

Thank you for reading this book. You will find it to be intentionally brief and to the point, with perspectives you can apply to all your business relationships immediately. I encourage you to share what you learn with the people you work with, the partners that extend your value, and the customers with whom you interact regularly. Use what you learn in this book to build collaboration and a common vision for building relationships in which you will invest, through the right channels, to create responsible, accountable, and transparent experiences.

JC

Part 1

"You say we have a business **relationship**? That is not what I would call it…"

CHAPTER 1

Recognizing Root Problems

In a business climate where silos are pervasive and seem unconquerable, attempting to bring people together under this notion of building serious business relationships through a common methodology may sound like a lot of work. You already have enough problems trying to get customers to connect with you, employees to work with one other, and alliance partners to compete fairly. If you cannot even solve these issues, how do you teach people to work together for the benefit of relationships for which they are not directly responsible? To benefit from commonalities that make a business relationship successful? The answer is (as we will discuss in length throughout the book) that the alternative could, and probably already is, disintegrating and deteriorating the relationships you currently manage. The results of overlooking relationship building as a core part of your business manifest itself through poor employee and customer retention. That, in turn, snowballs into revenue and resource issues that end up getting the attention and blame. Fortunately, the solutions to connecting with people and building a healthy business, as a result, are both based on skills you already have.

ASKING ABOUT SERIOUS RELATIONSHIPS

In a survey of 400 business professionals across North America, I asked participants to share their perceptions of relationship development at work (with customers, employees, and their other business associations). When asked if business needs come before building genuine business relationships, 98% of participants strongly disagreed. When asked if they believed that business relationships are built differently from the way interpersonal relationships are built, 70% of participants strongly disagreed. We then listed specific relationship elements and asked the same group about their "relationship skill level" within each area across both personal and work relationships.

We asked questions about the importance of fairness and equity, setting the right expectations, explaining the value of the relationship, and mitigating risks. We asked questions about clear communication, creating a climate that encourages participation, considering the channels people prefer, and listening with genuine intent. We asked about being mindful of the heritage and culture of people and considering their individual needs and beliefs. We asked about the importance of keeping commitments, showing empathy, taking ownership of mistakes, and even about the importance of learning the skills needed to make the relationship successful. Finally, we asked about the importance of consistency, integrity, transparency. The results were overwhelming. Over 98% of participants agreed that these components were of major significance to the success of their relationships inside and outside of work (with significant others at home as well as with the people they worked with and served in their business).

Participants were also asked to evaluate their relationship skills. Here are the results:

About their skills defining the relationship:	
Make it mutually fair/equitable	89%
Set correct expectations	75%
Explain the value of the relationship	55%
Explain how risks are mitigated	42%
About their skills creating engagement:	
Genuinely listen	85%
Create a climate that encourages participation	75%
Communicate clearly	68%

Consider the channels others want to use to communicate	57%
About their skills personalizing interactions:	
Consider what is most relevant to the other person	89%
Makes adjustments to accommodate individual differences	81%
Considers national culture / heritage	42%
Considers individual belief systems	38%
About their skills being responsible and accountable:	
Keep commitments	85%
Shows empathy	81%
Stays knowledgeable of what others need	74%
Takes ownership for mistakes	68%
About their skills building trust:	
Consistency between words and actions	91%
Integrity	87%
Communicates thoughts and intentions transparently	72%

Except for risk mitigation, and considering the importance of national culture and individual belief systems, most of the participants in our survey rated themselves very high. If fact if this were a representative sample of the average person at work, and an accurate demonstration of how people manage their business relationships, we would have an average of 71% of people doing all the right things.

But the survey does not end there. We asked another important set of questions. Questions about the reality of the work environment of the participants. When asked if the companies they worked for were genuine about their relationships with customers (specifically), over 71% strongly disagreed. When asked if they felt their relationships with work peers were genuine, 74% strongly disagreed. When we asked if they felt their relationship with their boss was genuine, 73% strongly disagreed. When asked the same question about managers and their relationship with employees, 71% strongly disagreed.

We are left with an interesting dilemma. More than 71% of participants believe they are doing all the right things, and 72% of the same survey participants say they do not see a significant level of authenticity in the relationships they experience with customers, managers, and peers. Other studies conducted elsewhere in the world show similar findings and discover widespread behavior that includes such destructive behavior as bullying, discrimination, nepotism, social ostracism and loafing, and organizational cynicism[1]. So, while people generally agree that the skills needed to build successful relationships applies to both personal and work relationships, and believe they apply those skills, most people do not believe it is impacting behavior significantly enough to see a difference.

GETTING TO THE REAL PROBLEM

There are two types of problems we face in business but in particularly to the issue of building serious relationships in business: routine problems and adaptive challenges.

"Routine problems may be painful, expensive, and frustrating, but we have the advantage of knowing what to do about them and how to work through them. We have, in other words, a routine for dealing with them.[2]"

In contrast with a routine problem, an adaptive challenge is a problem for which we have no ready solution, no expert we can call upon to guide us through. No clear way forward. We have, in other words, no routine. We know we're facing an adaptive challenge when we find ourselves in unfamiliar territory with no mental map of our predicament; lost in uncharted terrain.

When you try to manage your business relationships in isolation, (customer relationships managed differently from employee and partner relationships) you create adaptive challenges for yourself. You do this by making the incorrect assumption that what a customer needs to be in a serious relationship is different from what employees and partners need to be in a serious relationship with you. This thought extends to relationships with just about every other business stakeholder. The most common adaptive challenge you create by treating your business relationships so differently is rivalry. You argue that the customer comes first, so you point everything at your customer initiatives. Then you realize that (albeit that you cannot be in business without customers) you cannot run a business without employees either. If your business requires distribution, and you depend on partners to manage it, then you can't take care of customers without them either. This has been a constant source of confusion for companies over the years. They do not realize that this adaptive challenge does not have to exist at all.

In the business family of these three children, (employee, customer, and partner) companies teach employees and partners that the customer is, in fact, the favorite child. This is an idea we have come to accept because no one really wants to fight against the "customer first" mantra. The truth is that secretly your employees are already fighting it. They fight it when you cut their salaries and overlook their own needs to make decisions that favor customers when they are clearly wrong. There is a better way to manage your business relationships and it takes equity and openness to see how relationships really work.

This challenge of finding a common practice for building exceptional relationships across ALL your business relationship is not an adaptive challenge at all. On the contrary, we have at our disposal a reliable and proven guide to how we form and maintain serious relationships, and it is applicable and effective across all the relationships that build your business regardless of culture, demographic or technology preference. Building serious relationships is a routine problem you have been resolving most of your life. You simply have not learned to apply it to the business relationships that surround you. Like with many routine problems, shifting your thinking to apply these interpersonal relationship practices to your business relationships could be painful and will require you to be flexible. You have the skills and ability to do it. The secret is to focus on the right elements of relationship development, without giving in to the many misperceptions about business relationships. Let's talk about a few of them.

BUSINESS RELATIONSHIP MISPERCEPTIONS

This year marks my 26th wedding anniversary. Shelley and I fell in love and married with all the romance and dreams of every young couple. Eager to learn and grow together, and already indoctrinated by our parents that "men and women are worlds apart" in behavior and thinking, we purchased and read every marriage and relationship book available. First on the list of "must read" books we chose "Men Are From Mars, Women Are From Venus[3]" by author John Gray (an enormously popular book at the time). The book offered suggestions for refining relationships between men and women through a better understanding of their respective communication style and emotional needs. The notion is that men and women are so different that they might as well be from different planets and that if you can figure out the stereotypical nuances of the opposite sex, you can work more effectively to understand one another and be happy together.

Well, Shelley and I are not the stereotypical man and woman. Shelley is an NFL Sunday type of gal with little interest in high fashion. Me, ever the metro-sexual male, preferred to stay away from sports and have more shoes than my wife. I did not want a man cave. Shelley did not want to paint accent walls. Shelley did not cry watching romantic movies. I did (and still do if you must know). As the emotional sports widow husband of a woman who loves every sport known to man (and yes, I am including curling on the list), I realized immediately that we had to find a better book. Fortunately, we never established notions of what a good relationship should look like from the book, although we enjoyed reading about the humorous situations couples get into in their first few years together.

It turns out that there was a reason why Shelley and I did not conform to the stereotypes outlined in the book. Findings in epigenetics and neuroscience now argue that men and women are not born that different at all. At the least, men and women are no more different from two men or two women with unique emotional styles. Scientific research shows that societal and parental expectations and perceptions produce behavioral differences that develop increasingly into adulthood. Studies like the one published in the Journal of Personality and Social Psychology[4] even target Gray's book specifically saying:

"The common belief that men are from Mars and women are from Venus is really wrong. We are all from planet Earth."

Study authors Reis and Carothers from Washington University in St Louis, looked at previous studies, analyzing 122 different characteristics like intimacy and empathy in 13,301 individuals and found that, in general, men and women did not fall into different groups. Although gender differences on average are not under dispute, the idea of consistently and inflexibly gender-typed individuals is.

Since reading Gray's book, Shelley and I have read many marriage books together, attended numerous marriage seminars, and learned much about how relationships work. I am glad to see that more relationship authors focus on interpersonal skills you can use to improve all your close relationships rather than focus on gender stereotypes. Yet, I am surprised to see that a considerable number of modern methods for improving interpersonal relationships (not just marriages or romantic relationships) are still based on the "Mars and Venus" perception. It has infiltrated how we raise children, how we develop friendships with the opposite sex, and how we think about relationships as a whole. It has even made its way into how we perceive the abilities of men and women in the workplace. Many of these misperceptions are also at the heart of our business relationship strategies.

CUSTOMERS, EMPLOYEES, AND PARTNERS...

Oh, my... Why do we insist on seeing our business stakeholders through different lenses? It is as if we are convinced that each is from a different planet, requiring a completely different relationship development approach. I have seen the "Venus & Mars" analogy used a dozen times over the years: "companies are from Mars, customers are from Venus" or "employees are from Mars, managers are from Venus" or "suppliers are from Mars, customers are from Venus." All these, by the way, are actual titles of articles or books. Like the idea that men and women are planets apart in behavior and thinking, the customers vs companies, employees vs managers, and the customers vs distributors comparison are widespread in our techniques for shaping business relationships.

Contemplating this point of view, strategist and author Valeria Maltoni makes an important point in a June 2007 Fast Company article entitled (of course) "Companies are from MARS, Customers are from VENUS ." She says:

"Companies are rational, logical, and analytical. Customers are (or they seem to be) irrational, emotional, and conceptual. Companies want proof, measure, and surveys. Customers want to be delighted, feel important, and count. Companies are from Mars, customers are from Venus.[5]*"*

What makes this article different from some of the others I have referenced so far is that Maltoni goes on to ask why companies can't be more like customers (connecting to needs and emotions and feelings). With the abundance of experts presenting the operational value and business benefit of catering to the behavior customers plead (relevance, appreciation, and engagement) why are companies still not delivering it? The answer, in part, is that companies still think that rational, logical, and analytical decisions belong in business and are the real source of revenue. While emotion and empathy and equity are unreasonable expectations of the irrational customer mind. It is also a view about employees who have reasonable expectations about their health and psychological well-being, while the company focuses on the end of quarter results and is willing to break promises they made to the employee to accomplish them.

This misperception, that our business relationships are so different and require a different skillset from one stakeholder relationship to the next is only true in that circumstances vary from person to person. The foundational skills required, such as managing definition, engagement, personalization, responsibility, accountability, transparency, and experience are common across all our business relationships. This is the first misperception to overcome.

UNDERSTANDING HOW BUSINESS WORKS

Business needs DO come first, but not in the way you may be thinking. If your idea of "business needs first" or the despised "it's not personal, its business" has more to do with priorities than how business works then you have it all wrong. So many people think that because they are at work the rules of relationship building must be amended. That somewhere between your kitchen and the carpool you must turn off a part of you that only works away from the office. What is closer to the truth is that the business first mentality and the idea that you must be tough and focus on cost and revenue does not help a business. It instead deteriorates the cohesive business model on which your company is built and which cannot operate effectively any other way.

In 2010, Alexander Osterwalder and Yves Pigneur, supported by 470 business practitioners, wrote the book "Business Model Generation.[6]" I recommend the book to clients often because it does a great job of explaining how business really works. First, it paints a clear picture of what it takes to grow and maintain a successful business. Secondly, as Osterwalder and Pigneur describe the nine foundations of business, they also describe the relationships that help deliver that value proposition, through the right channels and resources, to the right customer segments.

Our misinterpretation comes when we view business needs only in alignment with the "cost" and "revenue" components of the model Osterwalder and Pigneur illustrate so well. To many companies, running a business means keeping cost low and revenue high at any cost. It means cutting expenses to meet revenue goals. Sometimes those budget cuts encompass employee and partner fringe benefits.

We have created cultures that not only cater to this mindset, but that justify neglecting customers, employees, and partners and limiting their ability to spend time on the right activities for the sake of lowering cost and increasing revenue alone. In our short-sidedness, we overlook the interdependence between ALL of the nine business model generation building blocks and the relationships that support them. We are not really saying that business needs come first at all. We are saying that cost management and revenue generation come first, above all the other seven elements required to make our business successful.

Without a strong foundation of key partners, key resources, and customer relationships, a company cannot succeed in delivering its value proposition to the right customer segments through the correct channels and activities. Without relationships, a company cannot maintain a strong revenue stream and cost structure. The Business Model Generation process has strong, natural dependencies between external customer relationships and internal relationships. Customer Segments, Value Proposition, Channels, Customer Relationships, Revenue Stream, Key Resources, Key Activities, Key Partnerships, Cost Structure, Revenue Stream, Key Activities, and Cost Structure are individual parts of a single business strategy. You cannot estrange the relationships that facilitate your business activities from the functions and operations they make possible. The model is not composed of nine elements working independently or a model in which customer relationships are separated from internal resources and key partnerships. It is a connected model in which all functions and relationships are interdependent, weaved into a single model to make it effective. Without it, you cannot run a successful business. It is still true that without careful management of cost and generation of revenue we cannot stay in business for very long. However, it is a mistake to think it possible to grow a successful business, which achieves its key business objectives, while ignoring any of the relationships at its foundation.

At many companies, these nine elements work in complete isolation. The "business first" approach puts companies at odds with one another. It creates silos by placing revenue generation at the top of the priority list and undermining the component(s) that do not appear to be meeting that need. When customers are making you money all is well. You invest in employees and key resources. When you are not making money, you decrease your investment in internal resources as if you think that taking the one leg from a table and placing it on the other side is going to make it more stable.

When you overlook your dependency on all your business relationships, you leave the people charged with managing the relationships in your business ecosystem to fend for themselves; trying all the while to justify their existence against your "cost/revenue" mentality. The result is what we call "business silos."

I find it disturbing that, although Wikipedia reports that at its peak in 1967, the stockpile of nuclear warheads owned by the

Unites States came to an alarming 31,265 warheads. And that it is estimated that, since 1945, the United States produced more than 70,000 nuclear warheads, which is more than all other nuclear weapon states combined. Or that although the Soviet Union/Russia has built approximately 55,000 nuclear warheads since 1949, France built 1110 warheads since 1960, the United Kingdom built 835 warheads since 1952, China built about 600 warheads since 1964, and other nuclear powers built less than 500 warheads altogether since they developed their first nuclear weapons (with thousands of nuclear silos all over the world, active and inactive)... that Oxford English Dictionary uses the following examples FIRST to explain what a "silo" is:

"It's vital that team members step out of their silos and start working together: we have made significant strides in breaking down that silo mentality."

The "silo" mentality is in large part the result of companies trying to manage function without seeing the importance of connecting the relationships that make them successful.

Why are silos so pervasive in our business climate? Because to run a business that believes it is all about reducing cost and increasing revenue, people are encouraged to focus on the survival of their own organizations, teams, and jobs. Companies set the bar high to meet customer acquisition and retention numbers without considering that it takes people to do that, and those people need the same level of commitment, engagement, and transparency that it takes to win and keep a customer.

THE CUSTOMER IS NOT ALWAYS FIRST

This stakeholder thread I just described, which runs through the nine building blocks of your business, is very real and powerful. Although we have been taught that the customer is the most important component of every business because without him/her there is no business, that is not the full story. This relationship thread that weaves through the fabric of your business foundation is interconnected and interdependent. Closer to the truth is that ALL your business relationships are equally important, and form a connection that, when broken, keep you from meeting business objectives in one way or another. We cannot disconnect one relationship or neglect it without hurting the others. What we have learned to view as three separate business relationships (customers, employees, and partners) are not at all separate or independent entities that live and function in isolation. At best, companies tend to see the relationship between these business relationships as "symbiotic," and they are more accurate about the use of the term than they realize. That's because in biology, symbiotically refers to:

"any diverse organisms that live together, but the relationship is not necessarily beneficial to both. Parasites, for example, have a symbiotic relationship with their hosts, but only the parasite benefits.[7]*"*

What a perfect description of companies where the customer benefits from service quality, attention, and investment at the expense of deteriorating employee and partner relationships. It is another version of the "business first" mentality that in this case gives preference to customer needs because they are the source of revenue. In this symbiosis (so common at many companies), we point everything at customer experience or service. Then we struggle to create employee and partner retention programs that deliver on the same promise of investment and value that we promise customers. We know they are needed, and we know that in the end happy employees and partners create happy customers. Nonetheless, you still feel compelled to choose.

So many companies end up in this impossible situation of conceding budget and program efforts aimed towards employee and partner advancement because customer needs come first. I am not talking about cutting down on customer service improvement to buy an air hockey table for the rec room. I am talking about employees losing their job because you are spending so much money keeping the wrong customers and pursuing customers to whom you really cannot deliver value.

The connection between business relationships must not be a symbiotic relationship, but a "corporate relationship." A corporate relationship is the mutually beneficial association of a "unified body of individuals (the corporation)."[8] It is corporate because to be corporate a body is formed to act as a single body although constituted by one or more persons. They are supposed to be together coherently and for mutual benefit. The corporate relationship formed of customers, employees, partners, distributors, and other resources, exists for mutual benefit. This idea, unfortunately, does not describe the way many companies treat business relationships. For that reason, we make a disconnected decision and implement processes that benefits one and hurt the others. The "losing" business entity then struggles to be perceived as relevant to the customer effort. When you can't prove that relevance fast enough, departments are eliminated, and people lose their jobs. To make your business successful you must see people as stakeholders in the same effort.

TECHNOLOGY DOES NOT SOLVE ALL

The business first and customer first mentality is critical enough maladies to oppose, and I am tempted to stop here before introducing the seven relationship elements I have been discussing. However, I think it is imperative to address the common trend of turning to technology as the solution to many of our human-based problems. This is tough for me to say since I have been a technologist for most of my career, but, technology does not solve every problem and it certainly is not the first step in building a common foundation for stakeholder relationship development.

We are experiencing a digital transformation of everyday life. However, the need for technological change is driven by audience evolution and the transformation of the media audience[9], not by the need for more technology. It is easy to become dependent on technology to solve your business (and business relationship) problems. We are a technology-dependent society. If you don't believe me, think about the last time you thought you lost your cell phone.

Mobile cyber security company Lookout[10] reports that when asked "how did you feel when you misplaced your phone?", 6% of respondents said they were "relieved", 7% said "sick", 14% said "desperate", and "over 73% said they felt "panicked." A similar UK survey[11] found that 51% of the 1,245 residents questioned said that they suffer from "extreme tech anxiety" when separated from their devices. On the business side, companies are becoming more dependent on the use of technology, especially as the availability of software as a service has become common.

It is easy to try to find technology to solve your problems as a first step, and many organizations do that without proper analysis of where business process and critical thinking should be a priority. The solution, while a more instant and expedient outcome at the time, may end up delaying the resolution of the core problem. More importantly, it may keep you from working through related issues and from applying the critical thinking required to resolve conflict and improve collaboration. Thinking that technology should be your first option for solving a problem, may be making your problem worse.

Foreseeing these technological changes and the necessity to teach problem-solving to students, the National Science Board Commission on Pre-College Education in Mathematics, Science, and Technology had this to say about the effects of technological changes on students:

"We must return to basics, but the basics of the 21st century are not only reading, writing, and arithmetic. They include communication and higher problem-solving skills, and scientific and technological literacy -- the thinking tools that allow us to understand the technological world around us... Development of students' capacities for problem-solving and critical thinking in all areas of learning is presented as a fundamental goal."

Robert Ornstein of the Institute for the Study of Human Knowledge says:

"Solutions to the significant problems facing modern society demand a widespread, qualitative improvement in thinking and understanding. We are slowly and painfully becoming aware that such diverse contemporary challenges as energy, population, the environment, employment, health, psychological well-being of individuals and meaningful education of our youth are not being met by the mere accumulation of more data or expenditure of more time, energy,

or money... We need a breakthrough in the quality of thinking employed both by decision-makers at all levels of society and by each of us in our daily affairs ."

Studies by the Journal of Technology Education[13] suggest that we have become so technology-dependent that many of the problems facing society are a result of advancing technology. Thinking specifically about how we use technology to address customer needs, I am not surprised. Customer Relationship Management (or CRM... also the topic of my first two books) has undergone serious scrutiny for many years. CRM, known more for the technology that supports it than the business strategy it represents, was developed to solve customer relationship visibility needs. Highly publicized reports by reputable companies like Gartner, AMR, and Forester, in collaboration with companies using the technology, revealed high implementation failure from the perspective of its users when asked, "Did it meet expectations?"

CRM is a valuable lesson for people trying to use technology to solve a problem (one at the heart of its acronym) without staying true to the goal of building relationships. Today many companies have abandoned the idea that CRM is for building relationships or that it is able to manage the important elements that help build and maintain them. You can find this scenario across your business. Self-help portals and automated assistant software intended to allow customers access to information become tools to promote less human interaction. Human Resources software intended to reduce the workload of specialists reviewing resumes results in qualified applicants never even being considered. Technology must be a servant of the processes that infuse critical thinking and relationship development.

If you are not convinced by the studies showing our inclination to start with critical thinking but then abandoning it for technology infatuation, consider this: most of the technology you use has been christened with the name of one of the seven relationship elements introduced in this book. Yet, these technologies do not promote the behavior encapsulated in their names/acronyms. Customer Relationship Management does not promote genuine relationship development. Customer Engagement Management or Employee Engagement do not promote connection and value co-creation, and Customer Loyalty Solutions do not always lead to behavior that compels devotion to a brand. The good news is that technology can be the ultimate enabler when you design them to define relationships more clearly and deliver on what relationships need.

EXPERIENCE IS NOT JUST FOR CUSTOMERS

The last item on our list of misconceptions that hinder relationship thinking is about something we call Customer Experience, or Cx. The term "customer experience" continues to gain momentum as a strategy for winning and keeping customers and improving the way they recommend your products and services to others. It explores the cumulative impact of multiple customer touchpoints over the course of your interactions with customers across the company. The disciplines that customer experience methodology introduces (strategy, customer understanding, design, measurement, governance, and culture) are a solid foundation for building programs that help customers become more loyal to your brand. I am a genuine supporter of companies that implement it and who recognize it as an important step towards customer centric maturity. This book does not, in any way, challenge the techniques or methodologies introduced by Cx experts and practitioners.

However, the concepts upon which Cx is based are not exclusive to customer relationships. I believe that we are missing an opportunity to benefit from what Cx has taught us about how customers perceive their experiences at three different levels: meeting needs, making it easy, and making it enjoyable. Could it be that we have stumbled on a measurement for relationship experience as a whole, applicable to all of the serious relationships of our business? Maybe even our interpersonal relationships?

In a February 2016 LinkedIn post , Chester Elton, author of "What Motivates Me" and the NY Times Best-Seller of "All In" makes a valuable observation about the great leaders with whom he has interacted over the years. Elton says:

"The very best leaders we've studied do share one thing in common: They care about their people just as much as they care about their team's performance. In that regard, they engage their employees in tasks with passion and an

overwhelming sense of purpose, and they encourage their team members to grow and develop. We've found most of these managers ask some form of two very basic questions, and they ask them frequently and with sincerity. The first question is: How are you doing?... All of which leads us to the second big question great leaders ask: How can I help?"

It is no accident that the questions that measure great experiences with customers are so aligned with what genuine leaders ask their employees and teams. The idea of asking customers about their needs and how you made it easy to interact with you is closely related to how successful mentors ask employees and business associates about their needs.

In a May 2015 Forbes (Leadership) article entitled "Why The Future of Work Is All About The Employee Experience," author Jacob Morgan writes:

"...over the past few years, we have started to see the emergence of the employee experience which is now something that many HR leaders and executives around the world are focusing on. Like the customer experience, the employee experience is what happens when an employee interacts with your organization. It starts with how they first find and apply for a job at your company and ends with how they leave and includes everything in between.[14]*"*

I am happy to report that this idea is catching on and that many organizations focused on customer experience are applying this thinking to employee engagement efforts. However, it is important that companies also acknowledge that employee experience is not subordinate or supplemental to customer experience but rather a synonymous endeavor.

OUR CARELESS MISUSE OF TERMS

There are words we use in our private life that we grossly misconstrue in business life. Words like relationship, trust, and loyalty are used to name technology and business strategies that never lead to genuine behavior. What we call loyalty management programs is often just a gimmick-based strategy designed to entrap customers into continuing to do business with your company. We reward them for a purchase with points and perks they can only use through more activity and purchases. Yet, as soon as they see a better price elsewhere they are not compelled to buy from you. As you will learn in the Definition chapter of this book, there are many different types of customer and employee relationships. People seek your company and stay for their own reasons. Still, what you call loyalty is not loyalty at all. Loyalty involves mutual support, allegiance to the relationship, and commitment. The type of behavior you see in Apple, Harley Davison, and BMW brand customers. The type of behavior you see from Zappos employees. If your goal is stronger relationships, richer engagement, and further transparency then be true to what those words mean.

GET READY FOR A NEW APPROACH

What does a serious relationship approach to business relationships look like when you dispense with all these misperceptions? When you use common practices for developing business relationships? When you make relationship development an equal part of your business strategy? When you view all your business relationships as equally important stakeholders? When you stop thinking of technology first and instead focus on more functional, accessible, and emotionally connecting experiences?

It looks like a unified, collaborative, and orchestrated version of the way you are managing business relationships today. Except that instead of making business investment skewed towards revenue, customers, technology, and customer-only experience measurements, you leverage these business elements to make relationships stronger. You define the relationships to which you can effectively deliver value. You learn the skills to provide that value with balance and equity. You mold experiences that support it. THEN you get more revenue, improve cost, increase technology adoption, and develop more accurate measurements for the experiences of all your business stakeholders.

A serious relationship approach to business relationships also takes a more centralized view of business relationships. It does not separate how relationships are built with customers, employees, or partners but instead uses common skills to build relationships with all business stakeholders. I intentionally use the word stakeholder because although our customers, employees, and business partners comprise our primary business entities, there are so many other relationships to consider. The serious relationship approach is a methodology that even extends to our personal relationships because they are also stakeholders. Sound organizational development considers the impact of our personal relationships in our business life and ability to do our job. Therefore, you must clear your mind of traditional b2b, b2c, etc., roles and think about relationship skills and dynamics applicable across all your business relationships.

Are you ready to put aside all your preconceived ideas and start building stronger and more serious business relationships? Maybe even improve your personal relationships in the process?

Part 2

"I want **clarity** on the **value** you provide. Help me understand **cost**, **risks**, and **rewards**. Show me it is fair and **equitable**..."

CHAPTER 2

Serious Relationships Need (1)Definition

Ask young children their thoughts on this fabulous thing we call "relationships" and you get some interesting answers[15]:

How do you decide who to marry? Kristen, age 10...

"No person really decides before they grow up who they're going to marry. God decides it all way before, and you get to find out later who you're stuck with."

Kally, age 9, adds…

> *"You flip a nickel, and heads mean you stay with him and tails means you try the next one."*

What do most people do on a date? Martin, age 10…

> *"On the first date, they just tell each other lies and that usually gets them interested enough to go for a second date."*

Why love happens between two people? Manuel, age 8…

> *"I think you're supposed to get shot with an arrow or something, but the rest of it isn't supposed to be so painful."*

Ask adults about relationships at work and the responses are more somber. The idea of business relationships is commonly defined from the relationship portfolio perspective. This perspective evaluates the market arena and identifies market segments on which your offering is likely to be successful: transactions, segment or value network, and the relationships between them. It is the starting-point for investing in the relationship portfolio conducive to the value generation of the company. In other words, a company focuses on the customers that need what they offer and aims to generate revenue from as many as possible for as long as possible.

However, it is in the execution of the relationship portfolio strategy that many companies fumble by taking the transactional versus relationship approach.

TRANSACTION VERSUS RELATIONSHIP

These two ideas, transactional versus relationship marketing have gained significant attention in the past few years. The transactional approach is focused on the cost of acquiring a customer compared to the customer's lifetime value, represented by how much a customer buys from the company. The relationship approach (or relationship marketing) considers creating value for the customer and in the process, creating value for the company (so it stays in business).

In this book, we explore the need to see stakeholder relationship as the core asset and bringing attention to the human connection. That's because monetary transactions alone do not keep customers coming back. They also do not keep employees at your company for long. We are moving away from labor-oriented practices for hiring employees, realizing that pay alone does not motivate them to stay. We are moving to an employee-engagement oriented culture that demands our understanding of how human relationships develop and deteriorate. It is no accident that our customer and employee relationships display a powerful need for relationship definition.

You may be struggling with these two ideas because you have

been taught that for a company to stay in business it must have a clear forecast of the cash flow customers produce. For employees, the incentive is also based on financials related to employee productivity and customer deliverables. But it is the realization that you do not have control of the decisions people make that should help you realize the importance of focusing on a Return on Relationship and much as a Return on Investment.

That is why it is so important that your make definition the first step in the journey to building serious relationships. It may be obvious to you that for a relationship to form, develop, and survive, the people involved must understand its essential nature. Yet, it is a lack of relationship definition that leads many business relationships into confusion, resentment, and ending. Companies invest millions of dollars in customer, employee, or partner relationships that do not reciprocate, and who see the relationship as purely transactional. You must define the nature and expectations of your stakeholder relationships before you do anything else. You must understand how you give and receive mutual value based on the type of relationship and where it is in the relationship development process.

RELATIONSHIPS HAVE STAGES

In a November 2014 article[16], the New York Times writes about a then newcomer to the online dating service scene, Zoosk. Unlike its competitors, Zoosk's 2013 $2.3 million advertising campaign did not focus on love or even romance. Instead, it promoted the slogan "First Comes Like," highlighting the importance of the moments when daters discover each other's endearing qualities. If you have seen the commercials for Zoosk, you may have noticed the message "Love does not come first" (much to the dismay of love-at-first-site believers). The dating service believes that unlike other sites like Match and eHarmony (which offer members a chance at true love) Zoosk emphasizes the need for people to "click." The Zoosk model is not about getting to romance right away as much as it is about figuring out if you should even make the investment of time and effort. Before you make the emotional commitment, you first must "click." You must make that initial, unemotional assessment that will help you determine the level of engagement that may or may not lead to future experiences.

In their book, "Close Relationships: Perspectives on the Meaning of Intimacy [17]" George Levinger and Harold L. Raush explain that personal relationships can go through stages and follow natural processes towards growth or deterioration. They explain how relationships, which begin with mutual attraction or interest, display some predictable patterns. Using the ABCDE mnemonic, Levinger and Raush explain in a theoretical, logical, manner the phases relationships go through.

- In the "acquaintance" stage, a couple may be in contact purely because of a mutual attraction or interest.

- In the "build-up" phase, parties engage in self-disclosure and become increasingly interdependent.

- In the "continuation" stage, lives become enmeshed and the relationship becomes consolidated.

- In the "deterioration" phase, the relationship may deteriorate due to an imbalance of costs and rewards, or a high number of risk factors.

- In the "end" stage, the relationship reaches deterioration that may lead the parties to end the relationship.

There are marked similarities between business and personal relationships in this definition process. We define a business relationship as "an association between individuals or companies entered into for commercial purposes and sometimes formalized with legal contracts or agreements.[18]"We say business relationships bind us only through the contracts we forge with one another to exchange goods and services. While personal relationships are formed by covenants based on needs like achievement, admiration, respect, affection, and love.

However, although the motivation for forming agreements and establishing relationships in personal and business may be different, how you cultivate relationships follows predictable patterns applicable to both. While the nature of the agreements you make in personal and business relationships differ, how you build relationships is very similar. In fact, business relationships follow patterns identical to those in the close relationships stages presented by Levinger and Raush.

GETTING TO KNOW YOU, GETTING TO KNOW ALL ABOUT YOU

Business relationships go through an "acquaintance" stage too. It is an acquaintance stage you go through when you interview and recruit employee candidates. It is the stage you go through as you qualify sales leads. You take partners and distributors through it as you learn about their resources and funding sources. The acquaintance stage in business relationships also starts with a mutual attraction or interest. Although at first, the attraction or interest may be one-sided (such as with prospects), the interested party aims to elicit enough information about the level or interest from the other party to determine if the attraction or interest is at least reciprocated.

At this stage, you risk making the critical mistake of investing in the wrong customers, employees, or partners. Not all customers are a good fit, yet companies invest in blanket marketing to win customers that do not align with their value proposition. The result is a relationship that never quite delivers value, increases risks, and costs too much to maintain (sometimes even more to end).

Not all employees and partners are a good fit either, but unlike customers (where you tend to invest in as many as you can to add to your leads bucket), you are a bit more careful with employees and partners at the acquaintance stage. You filter resumes more carefully and use automation more extensively. You interview them for competency and fit with company culture. Great recruiters and talent departments even focus on emotional intelligence qualities to make hiring decisions.

Obviously, when it comes to accepting a new business partner or distributor, companies expect more extensive due diligence. Selecting the right employees and customers still require due diligence and that you ask questions to determine if the relationship has a chance to evolve.

WHAT YOU MUST DEFINE

The most important qualifying questions you should be asking, applicable to customers, employees, and partners are:

- **Value questions:** *What value is expected, desired, unanticipated, and received?* Value is at the center of the decisions people make about their business relationships. It is an expected component that helps people decide to enter, remain, or exit any relationship. Sometimes it is not about cost. It is about the value that cost delivers.

- **Boundary and role questions:** *What rules/terms regulate this* *relationship?* People expect you to clearly describe the essential nature of the relationship in a way they can understand it. That includes clarity about the roles and boundaries of the relationship. Generally, these are included in formal sales, employment, and distributor contracts. When they are not you have to be proactive to ask questions about the level of effort, expected duration, exclusivity, and even expected level or formality.

• **Risk management questions:** *How do you plan to keep a balance in risks and rewards?* At the intersection of cost and rewards is "value" and people want to continually feel that they are getting value from a relationship. Based on their perception of value, people are often willing to pay more or risk more to get a greater and richer result. Cost and risks are an expected part of building relationships. However, when people perceive that the risk or cost of the relationship is too high they will reexamine their level of commitment to the relationship. A healthy sense of value in the relationship (getting value, adding value, feeling valued) maintain balance in the relationship. Remember to manage even the PERCEPTION of risk (the possibility that something bad or unpleasant will happen). At the acquaintance stage, where business relationships are not yet consolidated, people abandon the relationship simply from anticipated or suggested hazard, the probability of loss, or high level of susceptibility.

A clear definition of the relationship, its expectations, rules, and methods to keep it fair and equitable is the first step in the process of building serious business relationships. Many relationships do not get past this stage or are forced to the deterioration stage by dishonesty and even deception. Many people overlook (not maliciously) the risk of formalizing relationships (closing a sale, making an employment offer, or signing a partnership agreement) that do not have a chance for growth and mutual benefit.

The investment gets expensive regardless of who initiates the relationship. Companies all over the globe spend millions in customer acquisition and retention that never leads to a sale because they did not clearly communicate definition, expectation, and value. Similar investments are made in hiring and training employees who do not perform as needed or who leave shortly after being hired from a lack of clear skill definition, expectation management, and a mutual sense of value.

The remaining stages in the "close relationship" are also applicable to business relationships and we will discuss how they align with the "serious relationship" business approach in the following chapters. Keep in mind that the five stages proposed by Dr. Levinger are primarily theoretical and logical. It is difficult to see when or where one crosses the boundary between one phase and another. Therefore, I must emphasize that the idea of transitions among the phases may not be progressive or orderly. Sometimes acquaintanceships lead directly to the end of the relationship, or to consolidation without build-up much like the customer journey is not always linear and employment can happen directly without an interview. The model, nonetheless, is a rhetorical device and not always amenable to research. However, it helps us to visualize how relationships can move to or progress to other stages. The important thing is that we learn that these stages exist.

Before talking about the other six elements of successful business relationships, let's summarize the possible next stages of growth or deterioration beyond Acquaintance as you think of the definition component in the serious relationship:

- **B-Build-Up Stage:** In the "build-up" phase, business relationships engage in self-disclosure and become increasingly interdependent. Self-disclosure is important to the development of the serious relationship because it gives us access to the thoughts, emotions, and intentions of customers, employees, and partners.

- **C-Continuation Stage:** In the "continuation" stage, relationships become "enmeshed" and the relationship becomes consolidated. This is the stage that leads to closing a sale, hiring contracts, or signing up a channel partner. People formalize their agreements or show a formal commitment. Here is where you want your business relationships to go because here is where people begin to rationalize if this can become (or continue to be) a serious relationship. Consolidation is the foundation of strong, coherent, and effective business relationships.

- **D-Deterioration Stage:** Relationships that neglect one or more of the seven relationship components, almost immediately, begin to deteriorate. From here, a business relationship may deteriorate due to an imbalance of costs and rewards, or a high number of risk factors.

- **E-Ending Stage:** In the "end" stage, the relationship reaches deterioration that leads the parties to terminate the relationship.

Remember, this book is a guide to helping you prevent that and even provides steps for restoring business relationships that may have already ended.

"Facilitate a **positive communication climate**. Make engagement **engaging**. Build channels **relevant** to me..."

CHAPTER 3

Serious Relationships Need (2) Engagement

Before we talk about engagement... A wholehearted salute to the parents of teenage children! Having raised four already, and soon to raise a fifth, I admire parents and grandparents who achieve and maintain intellectual and emotional connections with their teens. Teenagers today are in their own world most of the time and struggle with tougher issues than those I had to deal with growing up. Engaging with them at a personal level is sometimes a huge undertaking. Good parents and teachers know that engagement is about more that relaying information. It is about truly getting through and finding ways to facilitate listening and participation in the conversation and its outcome.

It would be easy to use popular perception to make a point about how similar customers, employees, and partners are to teenage behavior when it comes to engagement (or a lack of it). I could say that customer engagement is difficult to attain and that customers have trouble engaging with the companies that so eagerly want their feedback. Companies do struggle with getting customers to complete surveys and questionnaires and participate in customer forums. I could also use the teenage comparison to say that companies also struggle to get their employees to collaborate in corporate initiatives with wholehearted support. After all, according to Deloitte's 2015 Global Human Capital Trends survey, employee engagement and culture issues exploded onto the scene, rising to become the no. 1 challenge companies face around the world. However, customers, employees, and partners are not like teenagers because teenagers are not as you perceive them.

Teenagers may get a bad reputation for being difficult to engage but that is not from a lack of need. The correct perception is that people (including teens) have a natural need for engagement and connection, but many of us (parents, service providers, and employers) do not understand what people need from us to feel comfortable enough to engage. If you are not getting the level of engagement you need from your business relationships, it is probably something YOU are doing wrong.

AN ENGAGEMENT CRISIS

In Western culture, we love to think we are relatively immune to interdependence; the type of engagement that keeps us from being masters of our own destiny. We think of successful people around the world, like author J.K. Rowling and Microsoft founder Bill Gates as loners[19] who did not need engagement to succeed. Surely, they did not need anyone to sway them to pursue their dreams. Both Rowling and Gates speak openly about their own personal needs for engagement and connection to other people. Other brilliant loners like Abraham Lincoln, Albert Einstein, Mahatma Gandhi, and Rosa Parks (who even titled her 2000 autobiography, "Quiet Strength") wrote about the importance of engagement.

The Deloitte Human Capital Trends study I referenced earlier says that...

"An overwhelming 87 percent of respondents believe the issue [of employee engagement and culture] is 'important,' with 50 percent citing the problem as 'very important'—double the proportion in last year's survey. Two-thirds (66 percent) of HR respondents reported

that they are updating their engagement and retention strategies.[20] "

Other studies[21] suggest that engagement improves hiring practices and deliver stronger customer service with lower turnover rates higher profit over the long run. Similar studies by Gallup found that fully engaged customers are "more loyal and profitable than average customers in good economic times and in bad." The findings are consistent across industries and target broad audiences, including b2b and b2c with strong links between customer engagement and key business outcomes.

Of customers, in particular, studies also show that...

"...a customer who is fully engaged represents an average 23% premium in terms of share of wallet, profitability, revenue, and relationship growth compared to the average customer. In stark contrast, an actively disengaged customer represents a 13% discount in those same measures. In short, when customers believe they are getting more out of a business, they give more to it. [22]*"*

Unfortunately, Gallup also reports that only 29% of b2b customers are engaged, with the remaining 71% either indifferent or actively disengaged [23]. Engagement is the key to successful word-of-mouth activity, recommendations, customer-to-customer support, and customer-initiated blogging and reviews that help you understand what customers need. So, when only 29% of customers are engaged, that is a very big deal.

Not surprisingly, a study of cloud resellers and other channel partners in 2013, surveying 215 channel partners in the U.S. (about 492 vendor partner relationships) shows that vendor/channel partner engagement is also perceived as weak and fragmented. The study shows that "one out of two channel partners don't think that their top three strategic vendor partners are doing a good job of soliciting their feedback on their channel partner programs, responding to the feedback, or acting on it."

ITS ALL ABOUT VALUE CREATION

Some studies of customer behavior suggest that customers who participated in the engagement process must feel satisfaction and trust [25] in the company first, and relations between the company and customers must first be strong. However, "blanket" trust (trust extended to the whole company) is not necessarily a requirement for achieving engagement. What is important is that companies understand what engagement is and what their business relationships expect from it; an elusive outcome called *value creation.*

In addition to the need for engagement itself, business relationships have in common the need to understand how their engagement creates value. Customers, employees, and partners alike share a need to understand the value that the engagement will create BEFORE they will participate. This is different from the need to understand the value of the relationship, which we discussed when we talked about definition. This is a need for understanding their participation in the creation of value as a prerequisite for engagement; how it extends, improves, or maintains value. Engagement is the tool you use to solicit validation of that value, but also the vehicle that creates partners in the creation process. Until people see the value it creates or supports, it is likely that they will not see the need or value for engagement regardless of who initiates it.

It is a brilliantly and simple fact that many organizations miss altogether. They miss it when they do not follow up on valuable recommendations from partners who want to improve the quality of products and services they sell on the company's behalf. Disengaged partners do not feel that their input is important to vendors. Companies miss it when they make employee surveys mandatory but then fail to empower employees to contribute and have a voice in those changes. Disengaged employees pass their disengagement to their customer interactions. Companies miss the truth about value creation when they bombard customers with surveys that do not explain how they will serve to improve the customer experience. Disengaged customers do not participate in customer forums and conferences and as a result, they feel that you are investing a lot of money to engage them only for YOUR own purposes.

The need for value creation is a reoccurring theme throughout each of the seven elements that create successful business relationships (and this book). Just as the definition of value builds a foundation for business relationships to be established, engagement keeps them "in gear." The word "engagement" literally means "being in gear." To be engaged means having great interest and presence of mind. It means being there with real interest, which leads to the creation of value. That does not describe what many companies call customer engagement, employee engagement, or partner engagement.

CHANNELS AND THE RIGHT CLIMATE

Achieving the kind of engagement that motivates your business relationships to collaborate is exciting and the type of accomplishment that builds exceptional companies. Just as it is important to communicate value creation, it is also important to create the channels and communication environment where it can succeed. Many companies ask their business relationships to communicate through the channels THEY (the company) see as important. Companies erroneously assume that customers, employees, and partners are ok with the communication channels you have given them to use. However, even though they may concede to using your channels to exchange information, you may not be creating the adequate communication climate they need to engage you or be engaged. Engagement is already a tough thing to get from people and if you ask them to use communication channels that are convenient for you and inconvenient for them you are obstructing the road to engagement. You are also creating a negative communication climate that may keep people from feeling that their preferences are valued.

It is tempting to hear the terms "unified communication" and "omnichannel strategy" and feel like they are the answer to your engagement challenges. Or that they, by default, create the right tone for a positive communication climate. The unified communication approach and the technology that supports it, as well as those for omnichannel communications, can lead to higher engagement. However, you must select the tools that your business relationships are telling you are most effective; the ones that make engagement easy for them. The right channels facilitate positive communication climates that lead to engagement, which leads to value creation. Remember, we are measuring engagement by asking if we made it functional, easy, and enjoyable. You want to create channels that reduce the effort for people.

ENGAGEMENT QUESTIONS YOU MUST ASK

- **Communication questions:** *Are we exchanging meaningful information?* One can never underestimate the lack of communication. Companies love to send customer emails, employee memos, and partner marketing without asking about their relevance. Companies expect customers and employees to provide feedback amidst through inefficient communication channels and processes.

• **Interlock questions:** *Do I create a climate in which communication can happen?* Communication climate refers to the tone and setting in which effective communication and engagement can thrive. A conversation through the right channel can have relevance but lack the attitude and tone needed for others to engage attentively and without friction. You have to help people feel eager to communicate and participate and co-create value. A positive communication climate makes way for creative dissent and expression that leads to problem resolution.

Remember that engagement is not a single act of connecting with someone. It is not engagement if it does not draw favorable attention, interest, and participation in the communication process.

"Show me that I am at the **center** of all your decisions. Consider who I am individually: My **values**, my **culture**, my **company**..."

CHAPTER 4

Serious Relationships Need (3) Centricity

Last year I traveled to Anaheim, California to attend a customer summit with a group of senior executives from a hundred different companies. I was fortunate to know many of the attendees personally. After dinner on the second day of the event, we began talking about a topic we all knew very well from the customer management perspective: *Centricity.*

The term centricity has been used for years to describe the need for companies to put customers first. As we began to assess how our organizations were doing, the topic began to shift to the importance of caring for employees and the impact of making employees feel like THEY were the most important focus of our businesses. We debated for a bit; each leader expressing strong opinions about the importance of empowering employees to deliver great customer experiences. Some stood firm for the customer always being at the center.

I had "gone there" a hundred times myself. Customers have always been a priority for me... until it came to making my team happy and to help them do their job. One of my favorite phrases, from author Michael LeBoeuf ("How To Win Customers and Keep Them For Life") is about the urgency of rewarding the people who make customers feel rewarded for doing business with you. No sooner the thought entered my mind I also remembered the hundreds of channel partner, ISV, and VAR events I hosted for software companies where I led alliance programs (or where I was a partner myself). I recalled making the same promises of personalized attention; to make their businesses the focus of ours.

Most of my peers at the dinner table at Anaheim echoed the same sentiment. That evening I learned a valuable lesson about centricity. That we all struggle to rank which business relationship should be the priority of our business, with most still affirming it should be the customer, but with reality telling us that they all deserve our individual attention.

It is important to acknowledge that, in spite of the prevailing customer-first perspective, companies have to address the close interdependence that exists between their core business relationships. That interdependence, and the importance of giving each of your business relationships the individual attention they need leaves us trying to find the right ways to define a fair business relationship approach. I have seen companies use mottos like "customer's first, employees second" to show customers how important they are, only to lose favor with their employees. I like the more balanced approach that Atlanta-based firm DENMARK (the Agency) takes with the expression, "customers first, employees always." It, at least, shows equal passion for the people they serve (externally and internally).

I am not debating the significance of your customers or the fact that they keep you (us) in business. Customers keep your businesses open and our families fed. No argument there. My emphasis is not that customer relationships should be LESS important, but that we need to stop being afraid of saying that ALL our business relationships deserve equal attention. Just as companies make the error of making decisions about customer relationships in isolation (sales, marketing, and support not having common insight about customer relationships), we also make decisions about our various business relationships in isolation. The people managing customers do not have insight into employee relationships and neither knows what the company is doing to manage partner relationships.

You have to stop fighting about which child mom likes better, and acknowledge that business relationships need equal attention and investment to run your business.

Tragically, many companies see their business as a train that carries as many passengers (customers) as possible (making a living from the fare). While seeing employees and partners as the fuel that gets passengers to their destination faster. The worse companies use their employees and partners like old locomotives used coal; tossing as much into the fire knowing there will be more coal waiting. Great for the owner of the train, and for the passengers, not so great for the coal.

Ask the question, "Who is the customer?" and people will respond depending on what they do for the company. We have internal and external customers who, from our perspective deserve personal and focused attention, no matter if they are a customer, a fellow employee or team member, or a VAR. To put it a different way, customers, employees, and partners are not the center of our business. People are the center of our business. At the heart of your successes and failures in business are your relationships with people.

In medical jargon, the term "centric" means "relating to a nerve center," which is an appropriate description of what relationships are to businesses. The word from which we derive the English word "centric" is the word "kentrikos" or "of the center," which comes from the word "kentron" or "center." Customers, employees, and partners are "of the center." They are not the center. The relationship is the "kentron" (center) of business. A company that focuses on the importance of relationships (rather than the customer or employee as the most important) is better equipped to apply the right practices across all its valuable business relationships. As soon as you begin seeing your business relationships in balance, you will also begin making balanced investments in the resources that make them feel that way.

When you begin to value relationships as such, you also learn to give the relationship that needs it most the proper attention without neglecting the others.

MAKING THEM FEEL LIKE THE CENTER

The many years of attention on the customer as the center of business focus is not necessarily a bad thing. It has resulted in an abundance of studies on the behavior of people and their expectations about centricity. In particular, the need for relevance and "personalization" stand out as primary expectation.

One of the most detailed and well-substantiated data I found on personalization comes from a 2015 survey conducted by Accenture Consulting. The Accenture Personalization Survey assessed customer expectations through a personalized shopping experience while noting the types of retail technologies, tailored customer experiences, and communications consumers may experience.

The survey results say, in part:

> *"To effectively implement personalization across all channels, retailers would benefit from understanding customers at a broad level as well as individually – determining where personalization strategies can best drive business results, and giving key subsets of customers the choice of how they wish to participate.* [26]*"*

The survey also showed that U.S. Consumers want a more personalized retail experience, but they also want more control (over 90% of those surveyed) over the use of their personal information. Even though millennials were more lenient in sharing personal data than Baby Boomers, they all expected companies to know them and their preferences better.

Returning to the emphasis on centricity being about all your business relationships (not just customers), studies on employee and partner expectations about personalization show similar needs. Studies of what motivate employees to stay with a company come down to a single conclusion: employees stay based on needs specific to them. They need to believe that you care about what is important to them and are willing to create incentives based on their personal needs and preferences. Similarly, the partner study we referenced earlier reveals that

"...resellers want to be asked questions that are pertinent to their particular challenges...instead of being asked the same old questions... [27]*"*

THE NEED FOR SIGNIFICANCE & RELEVANCE

Serious business relationships share personalization traits with interpersonal relationships and the behaviors that make people outside of work feel special. This is as much a business need as it is a human need for relevance, significance, and differentiation. Centricity is how you show people they are special, without having to say, "You are special because you are a customer" or special "because you are an employee." People want you to make it about them as human beings and about what is relevant to them.

Centricity is, at its core, how you make people feel that they are worth your attention. It is about how you communicate that they, individually, are relevant to your business. That their need is the most important matter at hand. To show people they are relevant requires you to ask questions about what your business relationships need to feel relevant. It also takes reorganizing your business around your business relationships. You must take a "relationship-influenced" approach that gives preference to the health of your business relationships, above financial and operational goals. This is where relationship building gets serious and demonstrable.

While it is not your responsibility to fulfill an individual's personal need for significance (unless that is what your business does), relevance is the most important aspect of centricity. You must consider how your personalization and centricity initiatives for employees, customers, and partners contributes to it (even if indirectly).

THE IMPORTANCE OF CULTURE

Remember the low percentage of survey participants in our business relationship study (chapter 1)? These participants rated themselves high on relationship competence in areas of expectation setting, value creation, and building trust but did not demonstrate the same level of confidence in addressing individual and cultural needs. Culture is an essential part of centricity because culture is at the center of who people are and what makes them who they are.

In the study of culture and its influence on business relationship development, we need to consider the impact of individual culture, national culture, and organizational culture. People bring cultural influences like their beliefs, values, norms, language, and assumptions about the world to their business relationships. Culture, in turn, gives meaning to the social structure of the organizations, groups, and roles where relationships develop [28].

NATIONAL CULTURE

National culture adds a second dimension to the relations development process in a business environment where intercultural collaboration and diversity is encouraged. I am not just talking about international companies. Within the United States, the US Census Bureau identifies 92 different ancestries that influence our economy and organizations. Most with strong regional influences and median household income over $60k. National culture is influencing purchasing decisions as much as how we make relationship decisions with our stakeholders.

In his comparative study of culture [29], Geert Hofstede describes the influence of national cultural framework across six prominent influences. As you read through them, think of the customers you serve, the employees that support your customers and one another, and the many other stakeholders that support your business. Are you considering the importance of national culture and heritage when making business relationship decisions?

1. **Power Distance Index (PDI)** - This dimension expresses the degree to which the less powerful accept and expect that power is distributed unequally. The fundamental issue here is how a society handles inequalities among people. People in societies exhibiting a large degree of Power Distance accept a hierarchical order in which everybody has a place and which needs no further justification. In societies with low Power

Distance, people strive to equalize the distribution of power and demand justification for inequalities of power.

2. **Individualism versus Collectivism (IDV)** – An individualistic society like the United States prefers a loosely-knit social framework in which individuals are expected to take care of only themselves and their immediate families. Its opposite, collectivism, represents a preference for a tightly-knit framework in society in which individuals can expect their relatives or members of a particular in-group to look after them in exchange for unquestioning loyalty. A society's position on this dimension is reflected in whether people's self-image is defined in terms of "I" or "we."

3. **Masculinity versus Femininity (MAS)** – The Masculinity side of this dimension represents a preference in society for achievement, heroism, assertiveness and material rewards for success. Society at large is more competitive. Its opposite, femininity, stands for a preference for cooperation, modesty, caring for the weak and quality of life. Society at large is more consensus-oriented. In the business context, Masculinity versus Femininity is sometimes also related to as "tough versus tender" cultures. It does not attribute any trait only to men or women but rather descriptive in nature.

4. **Uncertainty Avoidance Index (UAI)** - The Uncertainty Avoidance dimension expresses the degree to which the members of a society feel uncomfortable with uncertainty

and ambiguity. The fundamental issue here is how a society deals with the fact that the future can never be known: should we try to control the future or just let it happen? Countries exhibiting strong UAI maintain rigid codes of belief and behavior and are intolerant of unorthodox behavior and ideas. Weak UAI societies maintain a more relaxed attitude in which practice counts more than principles.

5. **Long Term Orientation versus Short Term Normative Orientation (LTO)** - Every society has to maintain some links with its own past while dealing with the challenges of the present and the future. Societies prioritize these two existential goals differently. Societies who score low on this dimension, for example, prefer to maintain time-honored traditions and norms while viewing societal change with suspicion. Those with a culture which scores high, on the other hand, take a more pragmatic approach: they encourage thrift and efforts in modern education as a way to prepare for the future.

6. **Indulgence versus Restraint (IND)** - Indulgence stands for a society that allows relatively free gratification of basic and natural human drives related to enjoying life and having fun. Restraint stands for a society that suppresses gratification of needs and regulates it by means of strict social norms. Think about these national influences for a moment in context with your business relationships. Think about the times when you

made investments to build a business relationship with a customer segment or specific company. Did you consider how their national culture may contrast with yours? How could they lack the same perception of fairness as you and your company? Think about your internal collaboration efforts and the times when you were insensitive to the expectations of more collectivistic cultures and their need for inclusion. Think about your cross-cultural projects and how your competitive spirit may have stepped over suggestions to apply a softer touch (or vice versa). When you realize the powerful influence of national culture on people, you build a stronger framework for building serious relationships.

ORGANIZATIONAL CULTURE

It does not stop with people. Organizations have cultures as well. Just as you must address individual and national culture in people-to-people interactions, you have to learn the prominent cultures of the organizations with whom you do business. Organizational culture is another area studied by Hofstede. In alliance with itim International [30], Dr. Hofstead has created a methodology and performance measurement that helps companies align organizational practices and national culture to create best culture performance. I am a big fan of the work they are doing and strongly recommend that you become familiar with it. Here are the elements of organizational culture directly from the itim International page [31].

1. **Means vs Goal Orientation** – The means-oriented versus goal-oriented dimension is, among the six dimensions, most closely connected with the effectiveness of the organization. In a means oriented culture the key feature is the way in which work must be carried out; people identify with the "how". In a goal-oriented culture, employees are primarily out to achieve specific internal goals or results, even if these involve substantial risks; people identify with the "what". In a very means-oriented culture, people perceive themselves as avoiding risks and making only a limited effort in their jobs, while each workday is pretty much the same. In a very goal-oriented culture, the employees are primarily out to achieve specific internal goals or results, even if these involve substantial risks.

2. **Internal vs Externally Driven Cultures** – In a very internally driven culture employees perceive their task towards the outside world as totally given, based on the idea that business ethics and honesty matters most and that they know best what is good for the customer and the world at large. In a very externally driven culture, the only emphasis is on meeting the customer's requirements; results are most important and a pragmatic rather than an ethical attitude prevails. This dimension is distinguishable from means- versus goal-orientation because, in this case, it is not impersonal results that are at stake, but the satisfaction of the customer, client or commissioning party.

3. **Easygoing vs. Strict Work Discipline** - This dimension refers to the amount of internal structuring, control, and discipline. A very easygoing culture reveals loose internal structure, a lack of predictability, and little control and discipline; there is a lot of improvisation and surprises. A very strict work discipline reveals the reverse. People are very cost-conscious, punctual and serious.

4. **Local vs. Professional Culture** – In a local company, employees identify with the boss and/or the unit in which one works. In a professional organization, the identity of an employee is determined by his profession and/or the content of the job. In a very local culture, employees are very short-term directed, they are internally focused and there is strong social control to be like everybody else. In a very professional culture, it is the reverse.

5. **Open vs Closed System** - This dimension relates to the accessibility of an organization. In a very open culture newcomers are made immediately welcome, one is open both to insiders and outsiders, and it is believed that almost anyone would fit in the organization. In a very closed organization, it is the reverse.

6. **Employee vs Work Oriented** - This aspect of the culture is most related to the management philosophy per se. In very employee-oriented organizations, members of staff feel that

personal problems are considered and that the organization takes responsibility for the welfare of its employees, even if this is at the expense of the work. In very work-oriented organizations, there is heavy pressure to perform the task even if this is at the expense of employees.

7. **Degree of Acceptance of Leadership Style** - This dimension tells us to which degree the leadership style of respondents' direct boss is being in line with respondents' preferences. The fact that people, depending on the project they are working for, may have different bosses doesn't play a role at the level of culture. Culture measures central tendencies.

8. **Identification with your organization** - This dimension shows to which degree respondents identify with the organization in its totality. People can simultaneously identify with different aspects of a company. Thus, it is possible that employees identify at the same time strongly with the internal goals of the company, with the client, with one's own group and/or with one's direct boss and with the whole organization. It is also possible that employees don't feel strongly connected with any of these aspects.

The core message I want to convey about centricity is "know people." Not just what they do or what their job is. Know them and learn what is relevant to them in the context of the business relationship you have with them. Know them at their very core by caring about their beliefs, language, values, norms, assumptions, and culture. Be a student of organizational culture and consider how they measure effectiveness, the role of employees and customers, work environment, leadership, and your organizational culture in contrast with theirs.

"Show me you have the **ability** and **willingness** to keep your commitments. Demonstrate both **knowledge** and **ownership** in keeping your promise..."

CHAPTER 5

Serious Relationships Need

(4) Responsibility

&

(5) Accountability

The idea of "service" runs through the fabric of everything we do in business. The good, bad, and ugly of customer service have brought us stories that range from the awful and insane to the humorous, heartwarming, and inspiring. You know what service is and how it works and the expectations your business relationships have about it. However, that may just be the problem when it comes to service as a characteristic, instead of service as a requirement of doing business.

The word service is so familiar within the context of work, that we overlook the balance its application requires. That balance tilts between our "responsibility" to do what we promised, and the sense of "accountability" required to meet that promise, and deliver on values like empathy.

THE NEED FOR GENUINE SERVICE

Serious relationships view "service" as a commitment to keep a promise at all costs. You expect companies to have a service organization that answers questions and resolves issues related to the products or services you purchase from them. Serious business relationships, however, expect that service organization to understand the importance and details of the agreements, what it represents to the person being served, and the personal impact it could have when those service expectations are not met.

Companies make promises to employees and partners about how they will resolve issues that prevent them from serving their customers and each other. Customers are not the only ones that feel the betrayal of a broken promise of service. Just as some companies violate their promise to deliver service to customers, there are many who break their commitment to employees and their sales and distribution channels. You may have experienced this yourself from an employer who emphasized their expectations about your level of service to customers and peers, but when things got tough financially failed to keep their promise to you.

They emphasize loyalty to the company and patience with their leaders when tough times come, but when the going gets tough they use layoffs as a way to stay financially solvent (even though studies have shown us that this practice is ill advised [32]).

The lack of service at any level of the company upsets the balance of business. When employees do not keep promises to customers, customers respond by not buying from you. When sales go down, some companies break their promises to employees. When employees feel that companies do not keep their promise, they leave, costing companies millions in training and onboarding. In the peripheral, partners are the face of the company for many businesses. They have extended relationships that make this circle of broken promises even larger. Like it or not, when a distributor or franchise of your brand breaks a promise to customers, to them, it is your brand breaking the service promise.

Hearing a customer, employee or partner complain about your service should be equivalent to them saying, "you broke your promise." It must hurt and feel as uncomfortable as when someone near and dear to you says it. It cannot be anesthetized by business talk or excuses about finances or resources. A promise made has to be, always, a promise kept. That is what serious relationships expect.

USING THE RIGHT MEASUREMENT

The word service is one of many words we misuse in business. It has become the label we use to refer to customer service activities and technology. As a result, we have stopped measuring service beyond the superficial anticipations of fixing something that is broken. When customers ask for service, on the other hand, their most basic anticipation is that you keep your commitment. Not just within reason, but that you keep your promise, period.

How we measure service (and that we have delivered service) has been the subject of debate for the better part of the past twenty years with many names for the initiatives that determine if a company delivered on service anticipations. This is an idea fully explored by Peter Hernon and Danuta Nitecki in their study of service quality ("Service Quality: A Concept Not Fully Explored"[33]) at Texas A&M University. The researchers noted that most businesses have an externally imposed requirement to implement service quality principles; an imposition made by customers who expect them to be responsive to that level of quality they promised. The study asserts...

"Fundamental to service quality is the need for cyclic review of service goals and objectives in relation to customer expectations."

This norm (that service fulfillment is defined by the recipient) and how you define what service is, has been adopted to employee and partner service perception as well. You use terms like "level of service" and even "service level agreements" (SLAs) when you discuss service expectations across all your business relationships. You have, for a while now, defined service across all your business relationships based on the measurements you use for rating customer service.

But are we using the right measurements? Specifically, we have defined service based on four metrics that measure how well we are doing to keep promises (or, at least, to determine if customers are happy): Excellence, Value, Conformance, and Meeting / Exceeding Expectations[34]. How customers feel about you based on these factors, you say, results in reciprocated behavior like repeat purchases and even loyalty.

There are positive and negative ramifications of forming our ideas about service on these factors:

1. **Excellence** is often externally defined. It may be a worthy aim but the definition of what "excellent" means changes dramatically and rapidly from person to person.

2. **Value** to some people means the quality of delivery as well as what the service is worth to them, individually, or to their company. However, quality and value are different concepts. Quality is the standard of something as measured against something else that may not be at all what you promised or even deliver actual value.

3. **Conformance** facilitates a precise measurement, but users of a service may not know or care about internal specifications you set to define service conformance.

4. **Meeting** or exceeding expectations is a nice thing to say, but it is an expensive moving target (perhaps even too all-inclusive). Because it is applicable to many service industries, expectations change and may be shaped by experiences with other service providers. The result is the creation of expectations you may never be able to meet, much less exceed.

I do not believe that we should have ever built our beliefs about service expectation using these four ideas to measure success, but we did. Books have been written that motivated us to "exceed" customer expectations and "delight" customers. We have implemented technology to manage our customer service and support resources to help maintain conformance to the matrix that kept us productive and operational. On the technology side, we have improved ways for customers to answer their own questions. Customers no longer must talk to a person to get answers. Now they can leverage the many communication channels available to them to get results. The technology is so effective, that people don't always know they are really chatting with automated attendant software that responds intelligently as the real service agent handles multiple other chats. Many positive things came from our efforts to be of service, efforts that also paved the way to better measurements and technology for employee and partner engagement efforts.

Here is the problem: Just keeping your promise isn't enough. People DO expect you to keep your promise of service, but their decision to continue to purchase from you or remain as an employee or partner of your company is based on something that does beyond the SLA. It goes beyond giving them the ability to help themselves or using automation to solve problems faster and more efficiently.

A BETTER MEASUREMENT OF TRUE SERVICE

Keeping a promise also requires thought, emotion, and intellect. We realize now that what authors like Michael LeBoeuf[35] wrote YEARS ago is truer today than ever: That when you make a promise to your business relationships, they expect you to be reliable, credible, consistent, responsive, and empathetic. Do what you promised... yes! Take responsibility for what you promised... always. Do it consistently... for sure. Show that consistency in your behavior, policies, interactions, and even the physical locations your customers visit and where your employees and partners work... no doubt about it. However, beyond that people also want you to show consistency in the methods you use to communicate with people and the message itself. They do expect you to react more quickly, especially since you now have so many additional ways to do it well (social, mobility, cloud, unified communications). So, what your serious relationships expect most is a genuine ability to understand their needs and feelings and act based on both your ability and commitment.

In recent years, we started to align the needs of our business relationships with their most basic needs as human beings. We are moving away from subjective measurements of service and we are asking the right questions about the right things. We are leveraging the psychology of human behavior at the most fundamental levels. We are applying it to how we do business with people at a global level. With customers, we are asking about experience, with employees we are asking about engagement, with partners we are asking about transparency (not exclusively, but we are asking the right questions). More importantly, what is the level of commitment to delivering on these relationship elements by being knowledgeable, responsible, and accountable? These are questions the serious relationship needs to be answered to transcend transactional thinking about what service really is.

Let's separate for a moment these two interconnected elements of service: responsibility and accountability. When a customer service agent is helping a customer, and reviews the service agreement, only to find that the customer is asking for something outside that agreement, the agent has two options. They can focus on the letter of the law and simply explain they cannot help them, or they can find ways to do what is reasonable to help them. When an employee is asked by another employee to help them with a project, and that project does not fall within their areas of responsibility, there may be no formal obligation to support the project but many other reasons to do so anyway. When a distributor asks for an extension of a delivery, you could simply put your foot down and read the terms of the distributor agreement or take the time to understand the situation. We are constantly at the interception of choices that involve responsibility and accountability.

The responsibility aspect of service is something you have agreed upon. You forged an agreement (legal, moral, or mental) to do something. With that agreement come expectations that you have (or will obtain) the skills and ability to meet that commitment with intent. Accountability is taking ownership of those responsibilities. It is "an acknowledgment and internalization of a sense of ownership for a task and the willingness to face the consequences that come with success or failure[36]." The serious relationship requires that you make these two often interchangeable ideas equally important. Without knowing what you are responsible for and taking ownership for the success of the relationship, even at the risk that you will have to admit your part in the deterioration and even failure of the relationship, you can't have true service.

"Give me **visibility** into your decisions. Keep your words and actions **consistent**. Give me reasons to build and maintain **trust**..."

CHAPTER 6

Serious Relationships Need (6) Transparency

I distinctly remember sitting with my daughter Reina in 1992 to watch the hit Disney movie, Aladdin. She was only nine years old (at the time my only daughter). During one of the initial scenes, Princess Jasmin, daughter of the Sultan of Agrabah runs away and ends up in the apartment of single, handsome thief and protagonist, Aladdin. As they are discovered by the palace guard (who had been chasing them earlier), Aladdin turns to Jasmin, hand extended, and asks, "Do you trust me?" A question followed by an Indiana Jones-like jump off the roof and into a safe canvas below.

A father's mind goes to strange places when it comes to his little girl, and mine went directly to this question: "Do you trust me? Are you serious?" I mean, she just met this dude!!!" Now they are all alone in his bachelor pad and he is asking her to trust him and jump off a roof together?

I feel just as aggravated when I watch TV or walk through the airport and see an advertisement from a company with whom I do not do business asking me to "trust them." The notion is like the picture I just painted of the princess running into the arms of a strange boy who asks her to jump off the roof with him. Perhaps my expectations should not be so dramatic, but it makes me wonder if companies even realize what they are asking when they ask customers to trust them.

Over the years, I have been fortunate to have recruiters approach me with fantastic career opportunities that did not materialize because of the expectation that I relocate to lovely cities like San Francisco, Miami, and New York. Moving to a new city to work for a new employer takes an even greater leap of faith. Not a week goes by that a friend of peer shares their own reservations about companies expecting them to accept a new position that requires relocation with little guarantees for the future.

When a business owner makes a financial investment in a franchise, they are not just investing money in a business. They are also investing their trust. Franchisees, channel partners, and value-added resellers trust the brands they represent to do the right things. They trust that the record of accomplishment that compelled them to make that investment will continue. When it doesn't, or when those brands make mistakes that tarnish their public trust, the damage rolls down to the companies and people that represent them.

This chapter focuses on transparency rather than trust for an important reason: serious business relationships begin with transparency, not trust. Trust is the outcome of doing the things we have discussed so far (defining relationship expectations, managing risks, showing value; facilitating engagement, value creation, and participation; giving people what they really need; keeping your promise. Being transparent in these areas results in trust.

THE CHOICE YOU THOUGHT YOU HAD

There was a time when a company could withhold damaging information (if even temporarily) with some hopes that, by the time people found out, they could formulate a plan for mitigating losses. Today, a single Tweet or Facebook post can take down an entire company, making its way across the globe in seconds. Overlooking the importance of transparency in a world where the smallest lie can be discovered and broadcasted to the world with such ferocity is not just bad business, it is reckless.

On the other hand, businesses that are transparent with their customers, employees, and partners can build genuine trust and improve the practices that build trust. The proverbial cooks in the kitchen are no longer hidden from site. People have a clear view into what is cooking and how it is cooked long before the food gets to the table.

This analogy came to life quite literally through a study conducted by a team of Harvard Business School and University College London researchers. In a Harvard Business Review Article[37], Ryan Buell, part of the research team, shares the experience. Over a period of two weeks, researchers set up four scenarios in real cafeterias where customers and cooks could and could not see one another. In one setting, neither cook or diner could see the other. In another location, only the diners could see the cooks. In the third cafeteria, only the cooks could see the diners. In the fourth, both the diners and the cooks were visible to one another. Buell explains,

"The results were pretty compelling: Customer satisfaction with the food shot up 10% when the cooks could see the customers, even though the customers couldn't see the cooks. In the opposite situation, there was no improvement in satisfaction from the baseline condition in which neither group could see the other. But even more striking, when customers and cooks both could see one another, satisfaction went up 17.3%, and service was 13.2% faster. Transparency between customers and providers seems to really improve service."

What a great object lesson on transparency!

Former employees of companies like HP, which eliminated between 83,000 and 88,000 jobs between 2011 and 2015, report transparency as an issue even greater than trust. Certainly, the layoffs led to a lack of trust in the company, but it is the lack of transparency into the intentions of the company which people reference as the source of stress in their relationship with HP even before the layoffs. The "Building Trust in Business," annual survey conducted by Boston-based Interaction Associates reports similar findings. In a survey of 450 respondents at more than 300 randomly selected companies from 2009 to 2013, the survey attributes a lack of transparency to the demise of trust, saying:

"...trust levels have declined every year (except in 2013) since the financial collapse began, with the largest drop coming immediately after the crisis hit. By swiftly (and sometimes secretively) executing layoffs and cutbacks, many bosses hid their company's problems from their staff, leading to a significant loss of faith in management.[38]*"*

Remember, the Dodd-Frank Wall Street Reform and Consumer Protection Act did not come from the generosity of companies willing to be more transparent. It came from catching too many cooks taking shortcuts in the kitchen. It ushered a new era of "corporate transparency" in which corporations are compelled to become more observable by employees, stakeholders, shareholders and the public. These regulations, and the self-implemented and self-enforced ethical rules of the pharmaceutical industries are a lot like the old church song about hornets. Hornets can't pick you up and force you to leave a room, but they sure can compel you to get the heck out of the room. From the perspective of outsiders, transparency can be defined simply as the perceived quality of intentionally shared information from the corporation[39]. Of course, that should never include trade secrets or information that takes away the competitive advantage and not something that jeopardizes health and safety.

THE ELEMENTS OF TRANSPARENCY?

No better word captures the idea of transparency than the word "candor." While transparency paints a picture of accessibility and clear sight into something, candor conveys the qualities of frankness and honest expression. Combined, the ideas of transparency and candor express both a willingness to let people access information to make decisions about you and your own willingness to be honorable and ethical in what you tell others. Creating a culture of candor is outlined in one of my favorite books on the topic, "Transparency: How Leaders Create a Culture of Candor" by Warren Bennis, Daniel Goleman, and James O'Toole[40] . What impresses me about the book is how it does not apologize for promoting the need for truth in our business and personal interactions. It does not try to explain the subjectivity of truth in business dealings or excuse companies for keeping internal troubles a secret from shareholders. It just promotes candor and telling the truth.

That simple message is missing from our business interactions and it is destroying trust in corporate America. I used some examples earlier when I described the way some companies hire people under false pretenses, promising a family like environment and a partnership for success when in reality their internal policies and secret board room conversations are promoting layoffs. It is way too common for managers to learn that they have to lay off an employee in a few weeks but not be able to tell them because it is "company policy" to wait until they can be escorted out the door. Surely there are circumstances where safety is a priority. Nothing wrong with taking precautions.

However, the most candid truth about why we do not tell people until the last minute is that we do not want the decision to impact the business. In that moment, we choose our own welfare and put the future of another person at risk. Why not be transparent? Why not be honest? Why not tell the truth? Because we do not see our employee relationships as serious relationships that were carefully selected and defined. Because we did not engage them to ensure clear communication and engagement. Because we did not take culture into account nor focused on responsibility and accountability in the business relationship. By this point, we think we must resort to a lack of transparency and hiding our true intentions.

I could share dozens of other examples where we do the same to other business stakeholders. We hide the true cost of doing business to win a deal. We intentionally give misleading information to buy us more time. We hide the truth. The most common reason (albeit inexcusable) is fear. Fear of the consequences of the truth. Fear that we will be embarrassed, ridiculed, or found out. Despite the literature on the neuropsychology[41] and levels of self-deception and the other studies on how deception exists in nature and social interaction, lack of transparency comes down to fear. What makes the lack of transparency tragic is that research shows conclusively that being honest and transparent yields greater benefits (including health benefits) than hiding the truth.

THE BENEFITS OF TRANSPARENCY

According to a "Science of Honesty" study presented at the American Psychological Association's 120th Annual Convention, telling the truth when tempted to lie can significantly improve your physical and mental health. In the study, Dr. Anita Kelly, professor of psychology at the University of Notre Dame, along with study co-author Lijuan Wang found that research participants could significantly improve their health by intentionally reducing how much they lied. Participants described their efforts to keep from lying to others and about being more transparent about their daily accomplishments. They discussed how they had stopped exaggerating, while others said they stopped making false excuses for failing to finish a task or being late to work.

The part of the study most relevant to this book is even more interesting: "In weeks when participants told fewer lies, they reported that their close personal relationships had improved and that their social interactions overall had gone more smoothly that week, the study revealed. Statistical analyses showed that this improvement in relationships significantly accounted for the improvement in health that was associated with less lying."

Transparency is the right choice not only for ethical reasons but because it benefits us directly in the most fundamental aspects of life. It helps us stay healthier and it improves all our relationships. The serious relationship requires transparency and candor.

"Make investments that help me get what I **need** with **ease** and **enjoyment**. Manage the experiences that build **emotional context** for me..."

SECTION 7

Serious Relationsips Need (7) Staging

I will never forget my first date with my now wife Shelley. I was a young, broke, enlisted Air Force guy about to take this wonderful girl out to dinner. I was a wreck. With limited funds and very serious interest in developing a meaningful relationship, I planned every second of our upcoming date. I borrowed a fancy car from one of my friends. I made reservations at her favorite Chinese restaurant. I asked to be seated close to the window where she prefers to sit. I took her to her favorite type of movie at her favorite movie theater.

I did not understand it then, but what I did that night was create an atmosphere where everything we have talked about so far in this book could take root. An environment that made it easy for her to get what she needed and where we could make an emotional connection. That night she made some assessments about the value I brought into her life and the level of interdependence she wanted with me. The environment and all my staging facilitated an experience.

THE IMPORTANCE OF STAGING

As I evaluate all the serious relationships in my personal and business life, I recognize this type of intentional and proactive staging that facilitated positive, meaningful experiences. It reminds me of the many business conferences I have attended and the marked differences between those that took the time to understand their audience and those that did not. The memorable ones felt as if every activity was designed with me in mind to give me what I needed, make it easy, and make the event enjoyable and memorable.

My son Jon, who works for an event staging company shares with me that a lot of work goes into these venues. The stages, as well as the seating arrangement, lighting, and vibe of the place, are all created for the artist and their audience. The staging constructed for theatrical performances can be just as impressive with its temporary platforms arranged to support performers who travel across the scaffolding to make their dramatic entrances.

In some cases, spectacular effects serve to introduce an actor or make a point. At the time, it seems unforgettable but then it is out staged by memories of the overall experience. Single events create independent experiences in which the audience immerses, but each event also becomes part of the perception of the event at large. They become part of the factors people consider when forming an opinion about the performers, the people upkeeping locations and equipment, the promoters, and the organizers of the event. They all serve a purpose. No element of the stage serves its own disconnected purpose. It serves to facilitate function, ease, and emotion that leads the audience to form a positive opinion and tell others about it.

In the development of serious relationships, experience facilitates functionality, accessibility, and enjoyment so that people can get what they need: definition, engagement, centricity, responsibility, accountability, and transparency. When the staging facilitates these relationship elements, the outcome is loyalty and trust.

Connecting everything you have read up to now:

1. You need to understand Definition because you need to invest in the relationships to whom you can deliver value and the expectations and boundaries of the relationship.

2. You need to understand Engagement because it determines

the channels necessary to communicate clearly and collaborate in the value creation process.

3. You need to understand Centricity to understand who people really are based on their personal, national, and organizational culture.

4. You need to understand Responsibility to perform your relationship roles with skill.

5. You need to understand Accountability to perform your relationship roles with ownership.

6. You need to understand Transparency to build and maintain trust.

7. And, you need to understand Experience to manage the environment in which all these relationship elements develop.

You can call it staging, or experience management, or just environment management. If you are evaluating how to remove physical and emotional barriers to serious relationship formation and development.

BEYOND THE EXPERIENCE TREND

The trend to manage experiences has evolved significantly in the past five years with a focus primarily on the customer experience. For years, Forester Research has been writing "The Business Impact of Customer Experience" report to help maintain focus on the importance of Customer Experience as a unique competency. As part of an online Q4 2013 survey of 7,506 US consumers about their interactions with 154 large US brands in a range of different industries, Forrester found a parallel between how customers rate their experience with a company and their subsequent choices to remain loyal. Forrester uses a measure called the "Customer Experience Index" (CXi) which uses three models to estimate the impact customer experience has on three loyalty measures:

- Willingness to consider the company for another purchase

- Likelihood to switch business, and

- Likelihood to recommend

The study shows that "the strong correlation between CXi and loyalty means that companies with higher CXi scores tend to have more customers who will buy from them again, who won't take their business elsewhere, and who will recommend them to a friend." Managing the experiences directly impacts revenue from customers who stay with you and bring in new customers. There is clear evidence of this. Books like "Outside In[42]" and the Forester research give us a powerful charter for managing the customer experience. They use meeting needs, ease, and enjoyment as criteria for measuring the success of customer experiences. This is a model, by the way, which many companies are also using to measure the employee experience.

However, I want to encourage you to make relationships your goal. Experience management must be the study and management of the environments that facilitate relationship development. While the concepts explored and implemented in many customer and employee experience programs is effective and something I support wholeheartedly, I want you to dig deeper into the human interactions that transcend transactional thinking. I genuinely admire the work of customer and employee experience pioneers. The practice of asking if a customer or employee accomplished their goal when doing business with you, if they didn't have to work hard to get what they needed, and felt good about it, are beyond question measurable instruments to achieve retention and recommendation to others. They are even good measurements in relationship development. I am not saying you should overlook them at all. I am simply encouraging you to evaluate all seven relationship dimensions. Serious relationships require it.

EXPERIENCE STAGING NEEDS

Each of the six relationship elements will require staging at any given time:

- To better Define expectations of value and relationship terms, you may have to create a safe environment conducive to honest conversations where you can resolve conflict.

- To achieve the level of Engagement necessary for people

to communicate you may have to invest in different communication channels and even create new environments. You will have to remove physical and emotional sources of friction that prevent participation in the relationship development process.

- To realize Centricity you may have to establish new affinity, customer, and partner groups. You may have to remove processes and policies that prevent the consideration and inclusion of cultural needs. You may even have to restructure your entire organization to create a relationship-focused culture.

- To increase Transparency you may have to remove physical walls as well as political walls. You may have to say goodbye to people who impede candor.

The decision of how to influence the experience will depend on the type of relationship people want to have with you. When we discussed relationship definition in earlier chapters we explored the need to understand the expectations of the relationship. While the focus of the book has been the development of deeper, more genuine business relationships, you will have customers, employees, and partners who only want to maintain a strictly transactional relationship. After all, customers do business with you for their own reason.

Employees join your company based on their own goals and needs (and those of their family and lifestyle), and partners build alliances based on their business goals. Interpersonal relationships work the same way. You have many relationships, each with varying levels of depth and influence in your life. The level of attention and investment you make in each relationship depends on the value you place on them (directly or indirectly).

RELATIONSHIP TYPES

I discovered a very interesting analysis of relationship types formulated by Carmen Lynch, M.F.C.C., a San Francisco-based couples and family therapist. Her approach was documented in a 2000 article by Victor Daniels, Professor of Psychology at Sonoma State University [43]. I will not go into detail as not a lot of research has been completed to quantify if relationships are structured under these types. However, the description provided by Lynch and Daniels looks very familiar to the types of relationships we encounter in business. The list is divided into five dominant relationship patterns and five collateral types.

SURVIVAL RELATIONSHIPS

Co-dependent. Symbiotic. Cannot survive outside the relationship. Parties can't make it on their own. Limited or no choices available elsewhere. Few shared interests or complementary qualities but still bounded by necessity. Often subtly or openly hostile and even abusive. In this relationship type, there is an imbalance of control. Despite all this, both parties are getting something out of it. This relationship type describes the relationship customers have with their cable and utility companies, especially when there is only one choice of carrier. It also describes company/employee relationships where economic and geographical factors limit the availability of employment. In both cases, it is common for the customer or employee or partner to leave as soon as a better choice is available.

VALIDATION RELATIONSHIPS

The relationship validates the sense of identity for one or more parties. It screams "You complete me!" Tend to be very insecure as they must be constantly re-validated. Theatrics and acting-out designed to get the other person to pursue you. There is constant testing of the relationship. One small act can turn into a huge validation or negation of relationship. Parties could be looking for different, even conflicting types of validation. This relationship type describes relationships with companies like Apple and Tesla in which customers seek brands that validate their values. In many ways, this is also applicable to the employee relationship at companies like Google. In both cases the brand is constantly validating the relationship, seeking input from the customers/employees and seeking its favor. It screams "Do you still love me?" In this type of relationship customers and employees are more loyal, if they feel validated by the company.

SCRIPTED RELATIONSHIPS

In the reverse, scripted relationships, the customer or employee is trying to conform to the ideas and image of the company or brand. It is more about living out the expectations for the roles they learned they were supposed to play. About maintain the illusion of perfection. Tend to get stuck in old patterns (this is how we have always done it). No trying new things or getting innovative. No system for discussing options for changing the way it is. Don't even try. Screams, "My way is the right way and I wish you'd just recognize it." Now, I am generalizing here, as I know these brands are indeed innovative and certainly listen to the needs of customers and employees and distributors. However, brands like BMW, Bentley, and Porsche set a standard that customers want to be part of. As a result, relationship expectations are set and people who want to buy or work for that company know what those expectations are.

ACCEPTANCE & INDIVIDUALIZED-ASSERTION RELATIONSHIPS

These three dominant relationship types offer rigid or partial control in relationship decisions. Or there is an imbalance of control in relationship decisions. The other two types, Acceptance and Individualized-Assertion, are more focused on trust, broader limits for making decisions, and greater tolerance of ambiguity. Acceptance type relationships represent what most of us want or assume a relationship should be. It is what you want from a service provider and the company that heavily recruited you with promises of a great working environment. The Acceptance relationship is open to work through issues with a more open mind and stretches the boundaries of a relationship to the borders of its limits. The Individualized-Assertion relationship type is more demanding. It is willing to make consensus IF there is an assertion of each person's wants and needs, based on respect for the other person's process of personal growth.

Here is the interesting thing about the five dominant relationship types: they provide a more defined starting point to make relationship decisions. You either have little control and focus on more transactional activities that support the relationship type already established (survival, validation, and scripted), or you have room to negotiate (individualized/assertion and acceptance types). More interesting still is that most of the work we do in business relationship development happens within collateral relationship types. Collateral relationship types are:

1. **Healing Relationships** – The employee, customer or partner had a period of loss, mourning, struggle, or stress before coming to you (or you going to them). This business relationship requires more validation about how your business practices are different from what led to their previous disillusion. Another company ripped me off. A former employer fired me unjustly. Another partner broke their contract and cause me a serious

financial loss. Healing relationships need Transparency more than all the other serious relationship elements.

2. **Experimental Relationships** - The employee, customer or partner is intentionally seeking something different from what they know or are comfortable with. They are trying it out. Many Dollar Shave Club and Airbnb customers are experimental customers. They have used traditional shaving products and are used to traditional hotels but are going to try out something new. For employees, this could mean working from home or an office or working in a new career field. The longevity of this relationship relies on Definition of value more than all the other serious relationship elements.

3. **Transitional Relationships** - A little bit of the old and the new. In this relationship, people do not jump into the experimental but rather try a bit of what they know and a bit of the unknown. This is the loyal GM customer who is open to trying a new connected self-driving car. Or the accountant who has been part of an established firm and now works for a small boutique firm owned by millennials. The transitional relationship needs lots of communication to make the adjustment and relies on Engagement more than all the other serious relationship elements.

4. **Avoidance Relationships** – In this type of relationship the customer, employee, or partner is avoiding specific behavior.

Perhaps because it caused them serious loss or pain. They protect themselves against the reoccurrence of same patterns and are therefore defensive and resistant to change. I have been hurt before. The avoidance relationship requires more personalization and attention to the cultural makeup of the individual and therefore needs Centricity more than all the other serious relationship elements.

5. **Pastime Relationships** – The pastime relationship type is the most uncertain as there are no long-term expectations. Here is where you can really put this book to use.

Stage the experience to provide a functional, accessible, and enjoyable environment for relationship development, accounting for the type of relationship you are managing. And as we stated from the beginning, assess the types of relationships you have the ability to invest in and support effectively. Managing every relationship of every type and trying to provide functionality, accessibility, and emotional context for all of them is both exhausting and expensive enough to put you out of business.

"… and I will give you my **loyalty**, **forgiveness**, and **endorsement**…"

CONCLUSION

Serious Relationships Need You

I hope you found this book valuable and that you have been able to answer the Serious Relationship question about your business relationship stakeholders. It is by first evaluating your investment in these seven relationship elements that you and your business will realize relationship benefits like loyalty. The important relationships in our personal life (our close relationships) get a lot of attention because, when they are not healthy, everything else feels out of balance. We seek to restore them at any cost because not doing so only perpetuates feelings of loss and the stress and emotional duress associated with it. We believe that if our interpersonal relationships are healthy, that we can tolerate anything customers and peers can throw at us. The reality is that millions of people around the world experience personal relationship loss because of the stress created by business relationships.

The challenges of maintaining a skilled workforce. The stress of meeting sales and service goals. The fear of conflict with distributors and resellers. It all adds up. It also all adds up to your ability to develop serious business relationships. Over 100 years of theory and empirical research on stress and well-being[44] has taught us that there is a correlation between stress and the quality of both our personal and professional relationships.

People want to understand the value, risks, and rewards of their relationships with you. They want to understand the rules and boundaries and expectations of the relationship in a clear, defined way.

People need you to communicate through the channels most accessible to them and that communication must be engaging and participative.

People need you to make them feel like they are the center of your decisions. The engagement I just told you about must be personalized to their individual and cultural needs. They must feel relevant and preferential in your decision-making.

People need you to understand your responsibilities to the relationship and obtain the knowledge and skill required to keep your commitments and agreements.

People need to know that in those times when you are not obligated to do something, that you still act with empathy and responsiveness. Sometimes people need you to be the better person.

People need accessibility and visibility into your decisions, thinking, and actions. Transparency allows them to see the level of consistency that leads to trust. And trust leads to the level of interdependence and self-disclosures that keep relationships together.

Finally, people need you to remove physical and emotional barriers that keep them from measurable experiences of definition clarity, engagement, centricity, responsibility, accountability, and transparency. When you deliver each of these six relationship components, ask: Did I give that person what they needed? Did I make it easy? Did they enjoy the interaction? Did I do everything I could to inject emotional context that helps them make decisions that lead to relationship longevity? If the answer is "no" to any of these questions, make every effort to improve until the answer is "yes."

ON A MORE PERSONAL NOTE...

Although my focus has been to enrich your business relationships and interactions with all your business stakeholders, there is a very personal message in this book. It is a message about improving the quality of ALL your relationships. Every one of the seven relationship elements can be applied to your interpersonal relationships as well.

You can use them to set clearer expectations with your significant others and identify where boundaries need to be set or restored (a requirement with your partner or spouse).

You can use them to have more candid conversations about what your loved ones expect from you and as a result make better investments of time and quality of that time through the right communication channels (a must for teenagers).

You can use them to explore areas of personal significance and meaning that make people feel like they are the most important person in your life.

You can use them to evaluate deficiencies in your level or responsibility and accountability to your role as a husband or wife, father or mother, friend, son or daughter.

You can use them to look in the mirror and with honest retrospection rate your level or honesty, integrity, accessibility, and candor.

These are the elements serious relationships require and the elements for which you must be ready to remove barriers.

Thank you for reading this book. Read it often. Share it with others. I value the opportunity to be part of your journey.

References

1. Jolita, V., & Jūratė, K. (2017). Forms of destructive relationships among the employees: how many and what the extent of the spread?. Independent Journal Of Management & Production, Vol 8, Iss 1, Pp 205-231 (2017), (1), 205. doi:10.14807/ijmp.v8i1.532

2. Weber, C. (2013). Conversational Capacity: The Secret to Building Successful Teams That Perform When the Pressure Is. McGraw-Hill.

3. Gray, J. (1993). Men Are from Mars, Women Are from Venus: Practical Guide for Improving Communication and Getting What You Want in Your Relationships. Harper Collins.

4. Carothers, B. J., & Reis, H. T. (2012). Men and Women Are From Earth: Examining the Latent Structure of Gender. Journal of Personality and Social Psychology. Advance online publication. doi: 10.1037/a0030437

5. Retrieved from http://www.fastcompany.com/931637/innovation-companies-are-mars-customers-are-venus

6. Osterwalder, A. & Pigneur, Y. (2010). Business Model Generation: A Handbook for Visionaries, Game Changers, and Challengers. John Wiley and Sons.

7. Retrieved from https://www.vocabulary.com/dictionary/symbiotic

8. Retrieved from http://www.merriam-webster.com/dictionary/corporate

9. Napoli, P. M. (2010). Audience Evolution: New Technologies and the Transformation of Media Audiences. New York, US: Columbia University Press.

10. Retrieved from https://www.lookout.com/resources/reports

11. Retrieved from http://www.thedrum.com/news/2013/07/11/over-half-brits-suffer-extreme-tech-anxiety-when-separated-smartphones

12. Ornstein, R. (1985). In A. Costa, (Ed.), Developing Minds. Association for Supervision and Curriculum Development.

13. Retrieved from https://scholar.lib.vt.edu/ejournals/JTE/v1n2/html/braukman.html

14. Retrieved from https://www.linkedin.com/pulse/two-questions-great-leaders-ask-chester-elton

15. Retrieved from http://www.daily-entertainment.com/archives/Kids-Say-Funny-Things/#.VsX8iPkrLcc

16. http://goo.gl/D6iPc0

17. Levinger, G. & Raush, H. (1977). Close Relationships: Perspectives on the Meaning of Intimacy."University of Massachusetts Press.

18. Retrieved from Merriam-Webster Dictionary

19. Retrieved from http://www.huffingtonpost.com/2015/08/15/famous-introverts_n_3733400.html

20. Global Human Capital Trends 2015, Leading in the new world of work. Deloitte University Press.

21. Great Place to Work® Institute, "What are the benefits? The ROI on workplace culture," http://www.greatplacetowork.com/our-approach/what-are-the-benefits-great-workplaces, accessed February 19, 2015.

22. The State of the American Consumer: Insights for Business Leaders report highlights findings from Gallup's ongoing study of the American consumer from 2008 through 2014.

23. Gallup Guide to Customer Centricity Analytics and Advice for B2B Leaders, 2016

24. http://searchitchannel.techtarget.com/news/2240219493/Vendor-channel-partner-engagement-is-weak-and-fragmented-says-survey

25. Banyte, J., Tarute, A., & Taujanskyte, I. (2014). Customer Engagement into Value Creation: Determining Factors and Relations with Loyalty. Engineering Economics, 25(5), 568-577. doi:10.5755/j01.ee.25.5.8402

26. Retrieved from https://newsroom.accenture.com/industries/retail/us-consumers-want-more-personalized-retail-experience-and-control-over-personal-information-accenture-survey-shows.htm

27. Groysberg, B. (2012). Talk, Inc.. Harvard Business Review Press.

28. Aronson, E., Wilson, T.D., & Akert, R. M. (2013). Social Psychology 8th ED. Pearson.

29. Hofstede, G., (2003). Culture's Consequences: Comparing Values, Behaviors, Institutions and Organizations Across Nations. SAGE Publications.

30. Retrieved from http://itim.org

31. Retrieved from https://geert-hofstede.com/organisational-culture.html

32. Robbins, S. P., & Judge, T. A. (2015). Organizational behavior (16th ed.). Pearson/Prentice Hall.

33. Nitecki, D., & Tiernon, P. (2000). Measuring service quality at Yale university's libraries. Journal of Academic Librarianship, 26(4),259-273.

34. Anderson, E. & Fornell, C. (1994). A customer satisfaction research prospective. In R.T. Rust & R. L. Oliver.

35. Leboeuf, M. (2000). How to Win Customers and Keep Them for Life. Berkley Trade.

36. Browning, H. (2012). Accountability: taking ownership of your responsibility. Center for Creative Leadership.

37. Retrieved from https://hbr.org/2014/11/cooks-make-tastier-food-when-they-can-see-their-customers/ar/1

38. Retrieved from https://www.entrepreneur.com/article/226673

39. Schnackenberg, A., Tomlinson, E. (2014). Organizational Transparency: A New Perspective on Managing Trust in Organization-Stakeholder Relationships. Journal of Management DOI: 10.1177/0149206314525202. Retrieved from http://jom.sagepub.com/content/early/recent

40. Bennis, W. G., Goleman, D., & O'Toole, J. (2008). Transparency : how leaders create a culture of candor. Jossey-Bass.

41. Trivers, R. (2011). The Folly of Fools: The Logic of Deceit and Self-Deception in Human Life. Basic Books.

42. Manning, H. & Bodine, K. (2012). Outside In: The Power of Putting Customers at the Center of Your Business. New Harvest.

43. Retrieved from http://web.sonoma.edu/users/d/daniels/lynch.html

44. Bliese, P. D., Edwards, J. R., & Sonnentag, S. (2017). Stress and well-being at work: A century of empirical trends reflecting theoretical and societal influences. Journal Of Applied Psychology, 102(3), 389-402. doi:10.1037/apl0000109

CPSIA information can be obtained
at www.ICGtesting.com
Printed in the USA
FSOW01n2222210617
35507FS